W9-BMO-767

Catastrophic Happiness

ALSO BY CATHERINE NEWMAN

Waiting for Birdy

CATASTROPHIC HAPPINESS

Finding Joy in Childhood's Messy Years

CATHERINE NEWMAN

Little, Brown and Company
New York Boston London

Little, Brown and Company
Hachette Book Group
1290 Avenue of the Americas, New York, NY 10104
littlebrown.com

First Edition: April 2016

Little, Brown and Company is a division of Hachette Book Group, Inc. The Little, Brown name and logo are trademarks of Hachette Book Group, Inc.

The publisher is not responsible for websites (or their content) that are not owned by the publisher.

Parts of this book originally appeared, in different form, on wondertime.com and nytimes.com; in O, The Oprah Magazine and in the magazines Brain, Child, More, Redbook, and Wondertime; and in the anthologies It's a Boy: Women Writers on Raising Sons (Seal Press) and The Cassoulet Saved Our Marriage: True Tales of Food, Family, and How We Learn to Eat (Roost Books).

"The Gods Watch Us Through the Window," from Tender Hooks: Poems by Beth Ann Fennelly. Copyright © 2004 by Beth Ann Fennelly. Used by permission of W. W. Norton & Company, Inc.

The Hachette Speakers Bureau provides a wide range of authors for speaking events. To find out more, go to hachettespeakersbureau.com or call (866) 376-6591.

ISBN 978-0-316-33750-2
LCCN 2015950313

10 9 8 7 6 5 4 3 2 1

RRD-C

Book design by Marie Mundaca

Illustrations by Peter Bernard

Printed in the United States of America

For my parents, who taught me love and worry

CONTENTS

PROLOGUE

IT GETS BETTER

You know how you feel when you see the RUNAWAY TRUCK RAMP sign on the highway? Like there must be an eighteen-wheeler barreling massively behind you, on the brakeless verge of destroying your beautiful, doomed life? You can picture the tiny, rosy-cheeked children screaming, clinging to you since you are, of course, riding in the back with them, the better to distribute string cheese and hand-holding and the occasional contorted breast, bared and stretched toward somebody's crying face, but only if they've been crying *for a long time.* About to be crushed—all of it. But "runaway truck" also feels like a metaphor for something. For you, maybe, with your impulsive desire to careen off alone to Portugal or Applebee's, just so you can sit for five unmolested minutes with a ham sandwich and a glass of beer. Just so you can use the bathroom *one time* without having a concurrent conversation about poop with the short person who has to stand with a consoling hand on your knee, looking worriedly up into your straining face. Later, it won't be like this. You'll see the sign, and the nearby gravelly uphill path, and you'll think, "That's a good idea, for the runaway trucks." Also, you will go to the bathroom alone.

You know how you know by heart the phone number of the Poison Control Center? Because the children, your constantly imperiled children, like to eat the ice-melting salt and suck batteries and help themselves to nice, quenching guzzles of cough medicine? One day you won't know that number anymore.

One day, the children will eat neither pennies nor crayons nor great, gulping handfuls of sand like they have a powerful thirst for sand, sand, only sand. They will no longer choke on lint and disks of hot dog or fall down the stairs, their heads making the exact, sickening, hollow-melon thump you knew they would make when you *knew* they would fall down the stairs. They will still fall out of trees and off of trampolines. They will still scrape their elbows and knees and foreheads, and you will still be called upon to tend to these injuries. And you will be happy to, because they will so rarely need you to kneel in front of them anymore, to kiss them tenderly here, and also here.

Rest assured, though, that there will be ongoing opportunity to be certain of imminent doom and destruction. Ticks will attach their parasitic selves to the children's scalps and groins. Rashes and fevers and mysterious illnesses will besiege everybody. You will still go on a Googling rampage of the phrase "mild sore throat slight itchiness coma death." The kids will still barf with surprising frequency—but competently, into tidy buckets, rather than in a spraying impersonation of a vomit-filled Super Soaker on the "Drunk Frat Boy" setting.

You know how you see germs everywhere? Every last microbe illuminated by the parental headlamp of your OCD? One day you won't. One day you will cavalierly handle doorknobs and faucets and even, like a crazy person, the sign-in pen at the pharmacy. Plus, in a public bathroom, the children will no longer need to touch and/or lick every possible surface. Seriously.

You know how you're tired? So tired that you mistake talking in an exhausted monotone about your tiredness for making conversation? You won't be tired. Or rather you will sometimes be tired, sometimes rested, like regular people are. You won't blearily skim the passage of the novel you're reading—where the protagonist lies down on her soft bed, between crisp, clean sheets—as your own eyes fill with tired, envious tears. You won't daydream about rest and recumbency, lawn chairs and inflated pool rafts and white hotel comforters. You won't look forward to your dental appointment just so you can recline alone for forty heavenly, tartar-scraping minutes. One day, you will once again go to sleep at night and wake up in the morning. You will sleep as much as you want to. You'll actually be shocked if you don't get to because a child is ill or can't fall asleep, even though now you lie wedged into various cribs and cots, night after night, still as a button, while a small somebody drifts off and snaps awake gropingly and drifts off again. "How did we use to do it?" you will ask, and your husband will shake his head and grimace. You will no longer be constantly scheming to lie down, tricking the kids into another round of Sick Patient, so you can be dead on the couch while they prod you therapeutically with plastic screwdrivers and the doll's bottle. "I'm still not better," you mumble now, but you will be. You really will.

One day, you'll be sitting on the couch with your husband, reading the Sunday paper, and around the time you're getting to the book review you'll think to ask, "Are the kids still sleeping?" And he'll shrug without putting down the sports section. The kids might be sleeping or they might be reading in their beds, playing with LEGOs, stroking the cat, bickering gently, resolving their differences. And you will be awake, *even though you don't have to be.* I swear it on a stack of attachment-parenting books.

Speaking of the newspaper: you will one day climb back into bed with the heavy wedge of folded sections and an un-spilled mug of hot, milky coffee. You will even do the cross-word puzzle—and all the puzzles you've been saving. It's okay. I know about the newspaper that still arrives constantly now, either because you're in denial about the way you recycle it un-read or because you cannot recall your account password and don't have the intelligence or emotional resilience to figure out the cancelling of your subscription. I know you still tear out the Sunday crossword and stuff it into the drawer of your bedside table with the crazy idea that you might get to it *later*. And you will. You'll open the drawer one evening (to ferret out some birth control, no less) and you'll find the archaeological evidence of your optimism: hundreds of puzzles spanning a sizable chunk of the early millennium. And you'll lie around doing them in a kind of leisurely, ecstatic trance, eating bonbons and weeping with happiness.

You will have time to run and bike and do yoga and floss and have sex. And sometimes you won't, but it won't even be the children's fault. It's just that you're lazy. Or doing a crossword puzzle.

You know your body? How it's like a baggy, poorly curated exhibit about reproduction? You know how your weaned bosom looks like a cross between a pair of used condoms and Santa's sack the day after Christmas? All empty and stretched out with maybe one or two lumpy, leftover presents that couldn't be delivered? It will all get better. The bosom will never again look like a bursting, gift-filled bag of awesomeness, that's true. But it will look less harrowed by motherhood. The breasts, they will tighten up a bit. All of it will tighten up a bit and be yours again to do with what you will. For example, your husband won't gesture to you at a party after you've been nursing the baby. "What?" you mouth back now, sticking a fingernail between your teeth. "Spinach?" He shakes his head and points at your front, and you look down to see the elastic edge of your tank top, and how your left breast is hanging over it. That won't happen anymore.

Even though you're older you'll actually be *less* hunched! One day, whenever you arrive somewhere, you will all simply get out of the car and walk inside! You won't be permanently bent over to deal with the car seat/seat belt/shoes/socks/sippy cups/diapers/turd on the floor. Why, you wonder now, does so much of your life take place *below* you? (It's because the kids are small.) One day infants and diaper bags and hemorrhoids and boobs won't be hanging off your person like you're a cross between a human mobile and a Sherpa and a performance-art piece about Dante's *Inferno*. The flip side is that there will be fewer cuddles. Lots still, but fewer. For example, every morning you will have to kiss your twelve-year-old good-bye not on the school walkway but in the bushes before you get there, like you're sneaky, chaste teenagers.

You know all those things you thought would be fun with kids but secretly kind of aren't? Going to museums, making biscuits, watching the Peter Sellers *Pink Panther* movies, ice-skating, swimming, singing in the rain—how they all end in tears and pooping and everybody needing to be rocked to sleep in the sling? All those things really *will* be fun! You're just doing them too soon because you're bored of Hi Ho! Cherry-O and the diaper-smell children's room of the library and those hair shirts of conversation about *Would you stay partners with Daddy if he turned into a mosquito and was always buzzing around and stinging everybody but had his same face?* One day you will watch *Monty Python* and *The Princess Bride* with the kids instead of *Arthur's Big Valentine's Day Guilt Trip* and *Caillou by Mistake Draws on a Library Book,* and you will hardly believe your good luck. At the dinner table you'll talk about natural selection and socialized medicine. You'll arrive at your campsite and the children will carry wood and play beanbag toss rather than cramming pinecones and beetles into their mouths before darting into the road to be run over by a Jeep. Your vigilance will ebb away until you actually take for granted how it feels to sit by the fire with a beer in your hand, looking unworriedly up at a sky full of stars with a lapful of big kid.

They will still believe in fairies. Sort of.

They will buckle their own seat belts and make themselves toast and take their dishes to the sink instead of flinging them from their high chairs to the floor like the drunk, tyrannical fathers from Irish novels. They will do most, if not all, of the important things that you worry they'll never be able to do, ever, such as follow the pendulum of your finger with their gaze and wade in the neighbor's inflatable pool and ride the merry-go-round. Speaking of merry-go-rounds: the years will start to fly by surreally, the seasons recurring like you're captive on a *deranged* carousel of time. The dogwood will bloom, it will be Christmas, the dogwood will bloom again, the children will start middle school. This is how it will be.

They will stop doing most of the annoying things that you worry they'll always do: they won't sob into their cottage cheese for no reason. They won't announce guiltily, "Floss isn't for *eating*," or make you sing the ABCs like a lullaby, *No, not like that, like this.* They won't ride the wheeled xylophone around the house like it's a skateboard or lick spears of asparagus before leaving them, mysteriously, on the couch. They won't talk about poop all the time. *Kidding.* They will still totally talk about poop all the time!

Not to be all baby-out-with-the-bathwater, but they're also going to stop doing some of the things you love. They will no longer imagine that the end of that "Eleanor Rigby" line is *all the lonely peacocks.* They won't squint into the darkness and marvel at the *moon beans* or hold their breath when you pass the *gravetary.* They will no longer announce odd questions into the darkness of bedtime. "Mama, Mama—how do cats turn into *old* cats?" And you will no longer sigh and say, "Time." But they will be funnier, and on purpose. "Is that a robin?" your daughter will ask one day, pointing to a bird hopping along the hedge. When you say, "No, robins have red breasts," she will say, "Plural? *Breasts?*" and use two index fingers to pantomime a bosom. They will make you laugh all the time, they will make you think, and they will be exactly as beautiful as they are now. But with missing and giant teeth instead of those minuscule rows of seed pearls you so admire.

You know how you secretly worry that this is it, that it's all downhill from here? I know you do. You worry that the children will turn into hulking criminals; their scalps will turn odorless. You lie in bed now during a thunderstorm, two sleeping, moonlit faces pressed against you, fragrant scalps intoxicating you, the rain on the roof like hoofbeats, heartbeats—and the calamity of raising young children falls away because this is all you ever wanted. Now you boo-hoo noiselessly into the kids' hair because life is so beautiful and you don't want it to change. Enjoy it. But let me tell you—you won't believe it, but let me tell you anyway—you will watch them sleeping still and always: the illuminated down of their cheeks, their dark puffs of lips and dear, dark wedges of eyelashes, and you will feel exactly the way you feel now.

Only better.

I

CIVILIZING

How to Throw a Tantrum

Birdy is two. She's tired, I'm tired, and our evening is turning into a series of trifling but cumulatively consequential moments, each one toppling into the next like the very dominoes of sanity. I'm not looking to cast blame here, but who invented giving up your nap when you're not even two yet? And who invented this frightful time of day? If I were the mom from *Bewitched*, I'd wiggle my nose and—*poof!*—one minute we'd be watching the sun just start to dip behind the trees, and the next the kids would be snoring in their beds. Instead I'm just mortal me with bodies to feed, teeth to brush, a pair of children to shepherd through day's end like sweet-faced little overwrought lambs.

First there's dinner. Birdy gobbles roast chicken while five-year-old Ben and I chew our food and discuss the "real pretend snake" a classmate brought to show-and-tell. There are smiles all around, the festive clinking of spoons and sippy cups, guitar music filtering in from next door. *This is great*, I think to myself. Like a fool. Because the very next minute is when Birdy decides that she wants to hold both the bowl full of steamed broccoli *and* the bowl full of French dressing we're dipping it into. "*I* hold," she says. "*I* do it." This would be fine, of course, if Birdy actually had a third arm. I love her feisty independence, but you just can't fight the laws of physics, especially the one that says: hold the broccoli *and* the dip, and there will be no hands left for dipping. She puts down first one bowl and then the other, then picks both back up and wedges one under an arm, trying to figure out how to grasp a broccoli floret and plunge it into the orange gloop without spilling anything or letting go of the bowls. She's a one-baby Laurel and Hardy act. This bowl, that bowl. That bowl, this bowl.

I am willing to let Birdy struggle for a while—I really do understand how important this is for growth—but finally I'm compelled to offer, "What if I hold the bowl of broccoli while you dip?" I'm just guessing here, but I think her screeching response means something like "No thank you." I've offended her dignity, and what follows is some obligatory stomping around, the accusatory groaning of the word *Mama*, and a few tears. But this is only, maybe, a three on the one-to-ten scale of toddler tantrums: *Loudly dissatisfied, but distracted by sticking fist into near-empty pudding cup.*

With the dip disaster behind her, the pudding blotted from her hair with a damp paper towel, Birdy now wants to "winse," which means standing on a chair at the kitchen sink holding measuring cups and funnels and every other available thing (including her own fleece-clad arms) under the running faucet, water spraying everywhere like our kitchen is a car wash. I say no to this now, even though I sympathize with the urge to drench, because it is bedtime and Birdy can never just "winse a *wittle,*" no matter what she might promise you. Again, a small fit ensues—"I *dooo* winse, Mama," she insists, along with the vague but emphatic "I *am*"—and Birdy stampedes up the stairs in a rage. But soon enough she is distracted again, wiping her face with her shirt bottom, singing "Itty Bitty Bider" and getting ready for bed. I breathe a sigh of relief—and then remember, too late, my superstition about sighing with relief.

Have you ever known a toddler? Then you understand how fierce and protracted a battle the simple act of toothbrushing can become. Birdy wants to do the toothpaste "by self" (it bloops out onto the floor); she wants to *eat* the toothpaste from the floor (she may not); she wants to clamp her teeth down on the bristles of the brush I'm maneuvering (this is annoying, and I tell her as much). She wants to suck on the washcloth I've used to wipe her grubby face (I let her). She wants to fish a dropped butterfly sticker out of the toilet with her hand (I don't let her). And, by the time we're done with the evening's hygiene, it's all been too much for Birdy—too much "No," too much "Stop"—and we approach something like a six on the tantrum scale.

I get a little snot on my shirt, in my hair, but Birdy pulls herself together. If my evening were a novel, or a *Jaws* movie, we might refer to this as "foreshadowing," and there would be ominous music to terrify you about the next ruinous ambush.

The real tantrum—the one you see slicing through the waves in the pointed shape of a fin—arrives a few minutes later, when we're already pajama-clad and snuggled under the covers for bedtime stories. Laura Ingalls Wilder's *The Long Winter,* to be precise. That's when Birdy finds herself unable to pull off her own fingers. "Aagh!" she cries, tugging on them. "Want to take dese fingahs *off."* She tugs some more, then she holds her hand out to me and says, reasonably, "Mama, help me, *bease."*

When I tell her that I'd like to help but can't—I trace her palm and fingers with my own finger to show her how seamlessly put together she is—Birdy throws herself down on the mattress and screams. The technical term for what's happening to her is "the last straw." She stands up again, still screaming, and with the tears riveting down her sweet face and her mouth opened into that red cave of yelling, she looks like a Beatles fan, in footie pajamas. "Fingahs *oooooofffffff!"* She's shrieking and tugging on her hands, trying to remove her fingers like they're gloves. (This scene feels oddly familiar. Was it in that tenth-grade film they showed us about LSD?) She bites into the comforter, tears at her own sleeve with her teeth. I don't say, "If you pull off your fingers what will you poke into your booty?" but I consider it. Instead, I say, irrelevantly, "Would you like to read *Fairy Went a-Marketing?"* and Birdy stomps away. Such a bald-faced distraction will not, at this point, be dignified with a response.

The thing about tantrums is that sometimes there is not only no way to help but also—and this is the kicker—no *point* to any of it. This is to be distinguished from the kind of tantrum that results from a disciplinary or safety intervention. If Birdy is about to plunge her hand into a Crock-Pot full of lentils—or if she's jabbing a thermometer into her ear or darting out into the road or hitting Ben over the head with *Pooh's Party* or spreading her cracker with ointment—and I speak sharply to her, well, the episode that follows always feels worthwhile in some way. Sure, the kicking and screaming are inconvenient, and you may have to stand in the middle of the sidewalk shrugging and smiling at the flinty passersby while your child flails a hole into the pavement with her snow boots. But righteousness is a raft you can cling to: an Important Lesson has been taught and learned, and yes, sometimes this learning is difficult and even ugly, but you really had no choice. But in "The Case of the Attached Fingers" there is no glint of a silver lining. Tiredness has simply forgone its usual, peaceful route (close eyes, fall asleep) and has instead taken a terrible, winding detour through paroxysms of fury and frustration (kick feet, bang head against crib bars). And the lesson "Fingers stay on" just isn't a very satisfying destination.

Meanwhile, back in bed, things have escalated. For instance, the word *bloodcurdling* pops into my head, and I actually picture my veins clotting up with purple lumps while Birdy rages on. And still, this whole entire time, I'm trying to read Laura Ingalls Wilder to Ben. I'm reading loudly, of course, so that Ben can hear me over the hand-wringing din of his sister. It's all a little surreal. Because here, on the one hand, are Laura and Carrie in a different century, stumbling home through a perilous blizzard to their worried parents—these courageous, uncomplaining little girls in their petticoats and woolen tights—and there, over there on the edge of the bed, is this gigantic baby flinging herself around and pulling her own hair because of her nondetachable fingers. Birdy's struggle is a real one, and her dear face is tragic and red and drenched. But when Ben makes eye contact with me, I raise my eyebrows and he giggles. Which is when Birdy staggers over with a pillow like some murderous yeti and presses it down over our heads. Under the pillow Ben and I are laughing and laughing: *Things are so out of hand.* When we come up for air, Birdy looks so sad and lost that I say, "Oh, sweetheart," and, against her will, take her into my arms.

I rock this person—this half-baby, half-child—and sing to her, a ballad about Spanish leather boots because those happen to be the only lyrics I can remember right now. Birdy is struggling still and crying hard, but I try to remember that sometimes, if I'm sad or despairing, Michael, my husband, might rub my back and speak soothing words to me, and even though he might not see any change on the outside—I might appear to be wholly and despairingly unaffected by his care—inside I am comforted. And just as I'm thinking this, Birdy's body softens in my arms and her screaming morphs into raggedy breaths with only a little bit of intermittent crying when she remembers her great Woe and Sadness. After the song ends, she sits up and asks, "Could I have tissue, *bease?,*" so polite that tears spring to my eyes. And when I hand it to her, she blots at her own eyes and blows her nose, smiles at me, and says, "Sink you, Mama!"

The thought that comes into my head is a cliché: it's like a storm passing. Birdy smiles, and even though the moon is peeking in through the tops of the trees, the bedroom is flooded with sunlight. And Birdy herself has the age-old impulse, the same thing I'm doing here, to make sense of her experience by turning it into a story. "I was," she tells us, her shoulders still heaving a little bit, "so, so sad." And Ben and I say, at the exact same time, "We know."

How to Throw Another Tantrum

If there were a Gilbert and Sullivan opera called *I Wanted to Suck the Dirty Washcloth* except there was only one line in it, and that line was "I wanted to suck the dirty washcloth," and the whole ensemble sang it while they were wearing just their Hello Kitty underpants—and crying—you'd get a pretty good sense of the most recent couple of hours of my life. Because there are rules, okay? You *can* suck the dirty washcloth— just not after it's already been flung into the dirty-washcloth bucket. Maybe it doesn't make sense to you, but that's the rule. Why do we have a dirty-washcloth bucket? Well, that's a good question. Like any normal family, we seem to use thirty-five dozen washcloths every day, and when they were all draped over the shower rod all the time, I felt like we were living in someone's back alley in a village in Europe. While it must be very charming to pass under a fluttering line of damp wash-cloths in the sunshine on your way to ogle éclairs at the patisserie, the way they were just hanging there in the electric light of my bathroom had more of a *shtetl* quality. Much better the washcloths should be festering in a large, white plastic bucket, as if we're actually running some kind of MASH unit. Much cheerier.

Birdy is newly three, and wiping her face is one of my favorite moments of the day: the way she turns it up to me like a ripe, smudged nectarine; the way I am my most tender, gentle self in this caring for her; the way I get to look at her with the kind of pure love that often, suspiciously, seems most profoundly to wash over me mere moments before the children will be asleep for twelve hours. Which is why I'm taken aback when, after I forget to offer her the washcloth ("Would you like to suck the dirty washcloth?" I think I'm supposed to ask) and drop it in the bucket instead, Birdy's head spins around and green vomit sprays everywhere, and a voice like electronic sandpaper says, "WASHCLOTH." Every single part of that is true, except for the green vomit. And also the head spinning around. Forget rinsing out the washcloth and giving it back to her, since this is as foolish a gesture as offering her a clean washcloth. You are obviously missing *the whole entire point.* Which is that "I WANTED TO SUCK THE DIRTY WASHCLOTH." *That* dirty washcloth. In the buuuuucket.

"You really wanted to!" I say, as she writhes and weeps and screams in bed. "You're so sad and mad!" This validating of her feelings is not as effective as one might hope. Birdy cries and cries the way you do when the only thing that can soothe you is the instantaneous snapping off of consciousness, which nobody else—except maybe a cartoon bird running by with a baseball bat—can help you with. I scratch her back. I sing her a lullaby. I stroke her sweaty, miserable hair. Ben reaches over to kindly pat her while whispering, "This is kind of annoying"—twinned impulses to which I can relate. This same six-year-old Ben who, one hour ago at *The Gondoliers*, the nonwashcloth-themed musical comedy staged by the fifth- and sixth-graders at his school, insisted on insinuating himself into my lap with Birdy after shuffling around and around, crying and miserable about the seating options afforded him (other, empty laps, for instance, or the mat where the rest of the kids were sitting) while the gaily beribboned gondoliers sang—some as charismatic as Elton John, others as slouching and vacant as Frankenstein's monster. Now, in bed, I say only, "Sometimes things are kind of annoying."

I say, "Birdy, you can lie here and cry, but the screaming is too noisy and Benny can't sleep. If you want to keep screaming, then you have to go in the other bedroom." And, screaming, she clambers off the bed, runs into the other room, and slams the door behind her.

Other times, Birdy's passions unfold differently. "Do you want some soup?" she asks me one afternoon. She's rattling around her pretend kitchen, shaking plastic pots and wooden vegetables while I cook real beans in a real pan. "No thanks," I say, because I'm a negative and distracted robot. "I mean, yes please," I add. "What kind do you have today?" She scootches all the pots over to show me. "Fruit gummy, carrot, or hot dog." "Hmm," I say. "I'll try a bowl of hot dog soup." "Actually, we're *out* of hot dog." She pushes the pot of hot dogs away with her foot. "Oh. Okay. Maybe the carrot, then?" Birdy's eyebrows pull together regretfully. "No, Mama. There's no carrot." Is she sneaking out at night to watch *Monty Python*? "Well, then, make it fruit gummy," I say, and Birdy says, "Okay!" She extends a plastic lid with one tiny wooden banana on it, holds it out on her palm, but when I go to take it from her, she wraps her fingers around it. "Actually? It's too hot. It's not really *warm*. I didn't really make yours yet. Here, give it to me." And she takes her fruit gummy soup and is gone again.

I feel about the children sometimes the way I used to feel about our tabby cat, Tiny. I used to look at him blinking slowly in the sun, or lifting his hind foot to chew at his toes with his minuscule front teeth, and I'd think *Why is he even living here with us? We have so little in common.* The thought was always accompanied by a cresting wave of love. "Our cat! Our dear, strange animal!" Our Birdy! Our dear, strange Birdy!

It's one thing; it's another. *The Popsicle dripped on my leg! My Lincoln Log house tumbled! A pen cap fell into the vent! Whaaaaa!* She's like a mood-changing specialty doll: push her button and watch her sunny smile turn to shrieking misery! Sometimes you'll discover that the indignities have actually occurred hours or even *days* earlier. Does Birdy sit around flipping through the mental files of injury and injustice until something strikes her? Who knows. Usually we encourage her to ask for the help she needs without first making a pilgrimage to the Wailing Wall and setting up camp there. Usually she does. There is more or less ado about something, and then she is able to resolve her frustration. Usually.

But on Washcloth Night, as on Attached Fingers Night, there has already been a series of incidents—I tried to hold her hand on the stairs; the Goldbug book is ripped (it was ripped when we got it two years ago); Birdy's head stuck briefly in the neck of the shirt she was pulling off—and finally the last straw came when I wet the washcloth to wipe her face, and she *wanted to do it myseeeelf. Eeeeeenh. Heeeeeeeee. EEEENHA.* She's crying still, we can hear her, and Ben is cross-legged on the bed in his striped pajamas, pale and chewing his top lip. "I think Birdy really needs you," he says, and he's right. I find her in my bedroom, trying to quiet her shuddering breaths. "I'm really pulling myself together, Mama," she says, and tries to smile, and I say, "You're fine the way you are, honey. Next time just ask for what you need so you don't have to waste all your energy being miserable." And she says, "Okay." I wipe the snot from her cheeks and kiss them, and I think about what a friend once said to me, as a gentle reminder against sloppy parenting: "We hold their hearts in our hands." And it's true. We do.

How to Be Afraid

It's bedtime in Amityville. We've been so completely lulled by our own placid rituals—a hypnotic "you are getting sleee-peee" piano CD, the children zipped into pajamas snug as cotton sausage casings, our collective recitation of the known-by-heart *Toby, What Are You?*—that the horror takes us by surprise. First it's the oscillating fan up on their dresser. In the half-light of evening Ben squints at it from his bed. "The fan looks kind of like a face," he says. I look at its round, blurred shape and hum a vague assent, but I'm the only person here who's half asleep; the children are both sitting up in bed now, wide-eyed as owls.

"The fan is making a loud-loud sound," three-year-old Birdy adds, as if we might be collectively cataloging the fan's attributes. "A loud-loud *noise*," she clarifies, and it's true. This fan is older than I am, dusty and belligerent, its blades clacking around in wavery circles.

"And it kind of looks like it's looking at me," Ben says now, worry hiking up the pitch of his voice. "Mama, will you please turn it, so that I can't see its face?"

Of course. Only something happens—the oscillator knob gets depressed somehow while I'm moving it—and the fan suddenly twists around, its old head roaring. Birdy screams and both kids dive under the covers.

Later, the fan is safely unplugged, and the children rush over to examine it with all the after-the-fact bravado of tourists poking a dead shark on the beach. The evening seems safe again, soporific even, now that the sky is fully dark and the frogs trill a little something from the pond, a croaky song about mosquitoes and the moon. But on the return to bed, fear shows up again, like a sudden knock on the door: Ben catches sight of his own distorted reflection in the window and startles. "Yikes," he says. "I know it's just me, but yikes."

"You're really having that kind of night," I laugh, and pull the heavy curtains closed, but when I go to arrange the sheet over him, Ben's heart vibrates under my hand. When our cat was still alive, this same thing used to happen to him at the same time every night, and we called it the eleven o'clock spookies—when one thing spooks you (a moth at the screen) and then another (the wind rattling the oak leaves), and before you know it, you're tearing around the house, your claws scrabbling on the hardwood floors, your own tail a menace.

I used to get it too, as a child, the bedtime scaredies. My own limb hanging over the side of the bed, for instance, could feel as inviting to potential fiends as a worm on a hook; my own pounding heartbeat could sound, to my ear on the pillow, like miniature marching armies. And were you supposed to turn your back to the bedroom door, which they could simply open and saunter through? Or to the crack between bed and wall, through which their miniature devious ranks could slip?

Maybe this is one reason we struggle with our children's fears: we actually understand them all too well. When the kids are afraid, our own weaknesses as parents feel embarrassingly visible, all our neuroses grafted onto the rootstock of our children. At any given carnival midway, I watch parents badger their trembling children, as though toughing out the Scrambler might be the key to human success—success cast away by any kid who just wants to ride the Baby Belugas again. People worry that their kids will appear weak or overly coddled; they want their kids to be "brave," even though bravery might properly refer to the righteous overcoming of obstacles rather than the simple tamping down of county-fair anxiety. I know how they feel, because at a summer birthday party, eight kids ran screaming through the sprinklers of a miniature water park while Ben wrapped himself in a dry beach towel and shook his head firmly—"No thanks"—and I encouraged him in nagging whispers.

"Don't get too attached," I want to say now—to the midway parents, to my own water-park self, to Ben. "These fears will come and go."

Because it's true—they will. For most kids, fear is a shapeshifter. One year Ben and I spin on the Tilt-A-Whirl together and I scream and scream, centrifuged flat like a screaming paper version of myself pasted onto the back of the ride, while

27

Ben smiles, as placid as a Cheshire cat. But then, even though his baby sister will, Ben won't ride the gentle carousel that summer. The joyless equine faces scare him. The next year he will happily board the merry-go-round and when a giant stuffed bear tries to embrace them, it's Birdy who bursts into tears. One year Ben says yes to the braining whiplash of the Rock 'n' Roller Coaster and no to the Haunted House; the next year it's the opposite. Birdy thrills to the flying elephants but dreads the spinning strawberries.

It's not linear, kid fear, and its windy path can be mystifying. In his six years of life, Ben has been variously terrified of: objects floating in water, lions, toilets that flush automatically, the blender, drains, bubble baths, death, crabs, dinosaurs, coconuts, school, dogs, crocodiles, elevators, Shrek, missing the ferry, snowplows, and snakes. There are some common themes — water, scary animals, loud sounds — and most of these fears fall well within the arc of reason. Some of them are even ones I share, in particular *snakes*. You know, and *death*.

Is Ben picking up on *my* fear? I wonder. "Catastrophizing" is the term I learned when I was pregnant with Birdy and a therapist friend of ours was trying to explain my style of worry, its calamitous trajectory. You see a runny nose; I see pneumonia. You see a splinter; I see an inevitable gangrenous amputation. Even something like an airplane safety card can set my heart to pounding: I picture the smoke, the blur, all of us scrambling after our seat cushions, clutching air masks to our children's faces, trying to remember if we were supposed to put ours on before or after. I don't even like to see a fire extinguisher behind glass: how is that eensy hammer supposed to work?

Happiness is so precarious. The babies arrived here suddenly, and I assume the snatching away of them could be just as abrupt. Our lives are held together with cobwebs, it sometimes seems, protected from shattering by only the barest coating of lacquer. A moment can be consequential. Slopes are slippery. One minute you're flipping through *People* magazine in a waiting room, the next you're getting a bubonic-plague diagnosis. Or one minute your six-year-old child is climbing on a structure and swinging from a rope, the next he's hitting the side of his head—*blat!*—against a pole and staggering over to where you're sitting with the end of a picnic lunch. And then he's confused and blinking for the ten earth-shattering minutes it takes you to imagine *coma* and *life support*. And then he's okay again.

But lately the news has been apocalyptic. I open the paper, and mudslides are burying towns, tidal waves are crashing over cities as if we're living in a sensational futuristic movie. We know too many young people with cancer. A family of four, friends of friends, have been murdered in their own basement for no apparent reason. *People just like us.* And one day, paused at a traffic light in the center of town, we catch the inexplicable sight of a gigantic snake, thick as Ben's leg, dead in the road in rubbery loops, its last meal a visible mess of blood and fur. It's so terrifying to me that it feels deeply symbolic—only I'm not certain what of.

"Where did that come from?" Ben asks, thrilled and panicky, and I have to say, "I'm not entirely sure." Other times he phrases the question more directly: "Are we safe?" I say, "Absolutely," and hope it's the truth.

Now, on this fright night, Ben has to pee one last time, and he talks Birdy into accompanying him. His latest fear is that a snake will slink out of the toilet bowl to greet his naked bottom—even though he knows that this is irrational. "Really," he reassures himself, "it would be drowned, and so the worst thing that could happen—and this wouldn't even happen—is that you'd flush up a dead snake. Which would be very surprising, although not exactly dangerous. But still." I know that "But still." I spend a good portion of my life there. Sometimes fear can be impenetrably shrink-wrapped inside its own logic, well protected from reason and reassurance.

But Birdy is Ben's perfect, fearless companion. "Benny's scared of the toilet snakes," she says gently as she toddles away beside him. "So I keep him company."

And Ben says simply and, in the best sense, shamelessly, "Thank you, Birdy." How beautiful they are in their openness, these kids. And in this moment I wish not only for safe futures but for what they have now: fearlessness about fear itself.

How to Have a Sibling

I don't always understand the children and what their problem is. How can you explain the arguments they have? Their primal irritation with each other? Tonight, for instance, they're fighting about who brushes teeth first. In contrast to such coveted operations as opening the front door or lying on top of me in the morning, toothbrushing is a situation for which the desired position is *not first*. "Who went first last night?" is the question every night, and, to be fair here, the children usually do a fine job of honest reckoning. I typically roll my eyes and wait, or I encourage one or the other of them to go first and get it over with—but tonight I am impatient and I intervene impatiently, not by helping them work it out, but by dictating, in the *dictator* sense. "Ben, you've still got your journal to write in," I say. "You first."

Who cares, right? It's toothbrushing, for cripes' sake. The ice caps are melting, the polar bears are suffering, wars ravage the planet, and here, under the microscope—what is that? It's an amoeba grunting, "I'm second!" A paramecium studying its foamy frown in the medicine-cabinet mirror. But it matters to the children. It matters to Ben, who consents to the brushing but has gone uncharacteristically silent with anger. It matters to Birdy, who—despite her coveted secondness—bursts into tears because, unwittingly, I call her in while she's in the middle of undressing. "Now you're going to see my *yoni!*" she sobs, naked and with a mouth full of toothpaste. "And it's my *private part!*" Private parts are serious business, so I say, "Go finish getting into your pajamas, then, sweetie," instead of "Um, excuse me, but weren't you the inventor of Naked Pilates?"

Oh, nobody will ever again be happy tonight! If these children were characters in one of Ovid's myths, their tears would spill over onto the tile floor until they drowned and became toothpaste-covered statues of themselves wailing. Instead they're just plain old tired flesh-and-blood children.

Why don't you make them a chart? is what you're thinking—which is a funny coincidence, because that's exactly what *I'm* thinking! "Hey," I say, and gather up the miserable loveys. "Should we make a chart about who goes first?" You can tell that I'm in real problem-solving mode here. I'm not normally a chart kind of parent because (a) In the Pol Pot school of parenting I attended, charts were rarely if ever mentioned, and (b) I prefer to work things out organically—to figure out the best possible solution at any given moment instead of determining everything in advance. I want the children to learn negotiation and compromise, and not rely on a set of arbitrary rules that were created to simplify—rather than, necessarily, to better—a situation. *Oy vey,* you are thinking now. *Quit overthinking everything and just make the chart already.* So okay, okay. I make the chart.

And the children love it. What is it about a chart? Maybe it's that it's so formal, like a reply card in a wedding invitation: *Steak or Salmon. Tom's Silly Strawberry or Colgate Too-Spicy Mint.* Or maybe it's that someone cared enough about you to make it. Or that life's vast existential abstraction is replaced by a little grid with your name on it. Or maybe it's that I'm so tired that in the first chart I make I switch the names every day but I also manage to switch the positions, so that I designate Ben first for every brushing. The children have never witnessed such hilarious buffoonery in their lives! Who but them has a mother so constitutionally incapable of making a simple chart? So tickled are they by the wrong chart that the right chart can only elevate their moods further. The children had not realized that I could produce such a marvel of efficiency and delight. They are thrilled.

Until morning. When they argue about who needs to get out of bed first. *Well, Birdy still needs to pick her sharing for school! Yeah, well, Ben eats breakfast more slower than me.* The problem-solving spirit of the night has evaporated into the mist outside. Am I supposed to make a chart about every single thing? *First brownie. Second serving of kale slaw. First good-night kiss. Second tick check. First inhalation of air. Second getting the barfing flu.* We can wallpaper our house with them. "Everybody up," I say, and pull my unwilling self out of their cozy, irritable tangle of arms and legs. "Get up. I am not going to make a chart about every single thing." And the children, like the good little soldiers they are, get quietly out of bed.

Some of life's lessons are self-evident, others easily taught, still others neither. Like another we've been working on lately, the one that seems tautologically apparent but turns out to be oddly elusive: *The problem with being annoying is that you end up annoying people.* Obviously. I mean, duh. And yet.

For example, Ben might like to comb my hair with a paper clip, and even though I'll say, "Ben, I hate that. I feel like you're going to poke my eye out," he just laughs and says, annoyingly, "Comb, comb, comb," dragging the bent wire through the tangles, a quarter-inch from my eyeball. "Comb, comb, comb," he laughs, and then, when I say sharply, "Ben!" he seems genuinely surprised: his eyes go wide, and he jerks his hand away like he's been slapped. "Honey," I say, and he says, "I know. Drive people crazy and you drive them crazy." Why do it? To combat boredom? Or is it the same pleasure as friction—the rubbing hard enough against someone that you can be positively, absolutely sure they're right there? Is it for the attention, even the attention of a person rolling her eyes or speaking sharply or, in the case of his sister, the attention of a person bursting into aggravated tears? Like when Ben switches the lids on the pretend food so that the tin of peas and carrots looks like the tin of gummy fruits. When Birdy says, "Wait, Ben, these aren't peas and carrots," Ben says, "Yes they are, Birdy! Look. It says *peas and carrots* so they must be peas and carrots!" *Peas and carrots,* it says *peas and carrots!* Until Birdy practically turns inside out with frustration. "Ben," I call, and he says, almost before I've uttered the one syllable, "I know, Mama. Birdy, I'm sorry."

The problem seems almost to be with the sharing of—how to put this?—*airspace*. The kids possess a unique and ongoing capacity to drive each other crazy, like an elderly couple who have been married too long. And are also hard of hearing. "Did Ben say *right?*" Birdy might wonder into the darkness of bedtime, and when Ben says, "What?" she replies, "No, not *what*. *Right*." And they will back-and-forth irritably with "What?" and "*Right*" for ten minutes—like Oscar and Felix from *The Odd Couple* performing Abbott and Costello's "Who's on First." There's just not enough room on the entire planet for these two to be alive in the same moment. In the morning: "I have a question, Ben. Ben—I'm talking. I'm talking first. Ben! My question is I LIKE TOAST." "You're interrupting. And, Birdy, that's actually a *comment*." In the afternoon: "I'm getting to the door first!" "No, me!" "Me!" "*ME!!!*" "Maaaamaaaa!" In the evening: "Birdy, move away from my dresser, please, so I can get my pajamas out." "Well, Benny? I *need* to stand here? Because I have hiccups and am hiccupping. It's my choice, Ben. It *is* my choice." Ben is entitled to his mild impatience, of course, but my heart clenches a little for Birdy—Birdy, who still tosses out utterances like handfuls of food into a fishpond where the fish aren't particularly hungry. "Honey," I say to Ben, "she's just making conversation, just talking. You can let it go."

Other times, they scream at each other, they scream for me, and they cry. I say, "Guys! Guys!" like I'm breaking apart scrappy basketball players. I say, "That's enough shrieking about the fruit leather wrapper!" like I'm in an absurdist documentary about myself. I say, "These people are driving me crazy!" like I'm being interviewed about office politics. And one surreally long day during a surreally long school break I say, "If you make it to bedtime without speaking unkindly to each other, you'll both get a treat." "What if only one of us does it?" Ben asks immediately—a letter-of-the-law attitude that will persist throughout the day.

"Birdy's telling me I can't come into the living room!" Ben yells from the hallway a little later. "Which really doesn't seem kind!" When I investigate, it turns out that she's orchestrating a pretend surprise Christmas for him, filling a series of her own socks with Little People and rubber finger puppets. "Honey, she's doing something *nice* for you," I say, and Ben, appealingly sheepish, says, "Oops!"

My disciplinary strategy seems to suffer from a lack of imagination. And heart. Because Birdy, who is much more loving than her brother but also more passionate, blows it by lunchtime when I overhear her say, "I will, Ben. I *will* scream just to drive you crazy. AAAAAAAH!" That evening when Ben picks out a Kit Kat from the treat drawer, Birdy sobs and yells. "I *am* kind!" she cries; she cries, "I *don't want to be* kind!"

Poor Birdy. Although mostly I think it's better to be second. Second kids blossom and spread inside that airy absence of scrutiny, while first kids are so often sweltering inside a kind of worried parental greenhouse where they get clipped into odd, neurotic topiary children. I don't analyze her every move as exhaustively. At least as a rule I don't, although I can still feel shame over her noisy and ardent behavior. Shame that I'm ashamed of. One day last week, when Birdy started moaning in front of my parents about eggs and not eating them and I, simply because I don't like her to be moaning in front of my parents (because I am, though second-born, an odd and neurotic topiary child), hissed right into her ear, "If you keep whining and yelling, there won't be any treats for you today." And she wiped at her eyes with the flat backs of her hands, pulled her mouth into an umbrella of sadness, and made not another sound.

We have so much power, don't we? The kids are in its thrall. We can change the expression of their feelings with a single command—but oh, it's those feelings themselves that I worry about, that silent turned-down mouth, the stifling need to be good, the way dependence can humiliate them. I don't know what the right thing is sometimes. But then I was wiping Birdy's face with a washcloth—gentling off that crust of dirt and tomatoes and dried tears and blueberries—and I said, "This was my washcloth when I was a little girl just like you." And Birdy looked at it—the wide Marimekko print of blue and yellow flowers—and said, "Did I wash your face so, so gently then?" I said, "When?" And she said, "When I was the mama and you were my little girl?" Then, like karma incarnate, she popped up onto her toes and kissed me on the forehead.

How to Eat Corn Bread

Here at the dinner table, Birdy is in an ecstasy of corn bread. It has dissolved inside her mouth into a curious paste, and she works it around and around, finally extruding a pale tube of it from between her lips like she's a coin-op polenta machine. "Oh, Birdy honey," I say. "I don't want you to do that." "Why not, Mama?" This is Ben now; Birdy can't speak for slurping the mush back into her mouth. "Is it not *safe*—like she could choke on it? Or not *kind?*" Safe and Kind is the rule at the kids' school. "Well," I say. "I guess it's that it's not kind, in a way. I mean, it's not *un*kind exactly—Birdy's not trying to be mean. But it's gross, which means that it disturbs the other people at the table." Ben considers this while he chews a mouthful of chili, as cautiously tight-lipped now as someone's old granny. He swallows, blots his lips with a napkin, then asks, "But why is it even gross?"

Sometimes I tire of answering their questions, it's true, but I love the way the kids keep us honest with their curiosity. Especially about manners, which can seem so arbitrary but, at their best, aren't. "Why?" is just such a good question. *Why do you have to say "please"?* Because it makes people feel good about helping you. *Why do you have to say "thank you"?* Because it shows people that you noticed them doing something for you. *Why do you have to use the forks in that particular order?* Because you're having dinner with the queen. Ben's like an etiquette sociologist. "Thank you, Mama," I cue into the silence after pouring him a glass of milk, and he repeats it absently. But then he asks, "But, Mama? I don't even really *like* milk. I drink it because you guys say I should. Do I still have to say *thank you* even if you're giving me something I don't even want?" "That's such a good question," I say, and mean it. "But yes, honey. You do. Society works best when people are as nice to each other as they can be." "I don't know," he ponders aloud, and I don't know either.

He returns to pondering when we're getting ready for bed and I say to a rascally-mood Birdy, "Please don't bite me when I'm trying to take your socks off." "You know, Mama," Ben says, "I think if what you're saying is *don't bite me* you shouldn't really have to say *please*." "Good point," I say.

We are strict about manners: the kids have been scolded in the car more than once, have returned, scolded and solemn-faced, to people's doorsteps to say, "Thank you for having me." When the veggies get passed around the table, I use the trick a friend taught me: "Brussels sprouts: *Yes please* or *No thank you?*" —(*Gag me* is not one of the choices, as I am quick to remind their father)—and it works like a charm. Overall, the children behave graciously, and their good manners are their own reward. "What polite children!" people gush at them in the hardware store, at restaurants, when they stop by my office—and the kids beam with pride. "Thank you!" they say, like caricatures of polite children. I don't mention the power struggles when they were toddlers—the standoffs over markers and cheese, when the little tyrants simply could not bring themselves to dilute their delight, urgency, or rage with the word *please*.

And Birdy can still, at three, turn petty and despotic:

"I need a wet tissue!" she cries, from her car seat, where an apricot fruit leather has stuck her fingers together. I wait to see if she'll catch herself.

"Mom, I said *I need a wet tissue!*"

"I hear you," I say. "It sounds like you really need a wet tissue!"

"I do!"

Silence.

"Mama! My hands are sticky!"

"It sounds like you've got some sticky hands!"

More silence.

"Mom, would you please get me a wet tissue?"

"I'd be happy to."

Part of what's difficult for preschoolers, of course, is that politeness is most often required when somebody does something for you—and three-year-olds don't want you to do anything for them. This morning we were watching Birdy wrestle with the large Tupperware container that houses her Playmobil figurines. "Unh," she groaned. "Ugh. Oof." "Here," Ben said. "Let me help you." But Birdy shrieked, "No, Ben! Don't." And then—just as he was beginning to lecture her ("Birdy, even if you don't want my help, you've got to...")—she corrected herself. "I mean *No thank you, maybe later.*" She darted away to the kitchen and returned with a spoon, with which she set to crowbarring the lid, and Ben turned to me with the raised-eyebrow gesture that stands in for ironic commentary about Birdy's likelihood of success. But when the lid finally popped off and Birdy hopped up and down triumphantly ("Yay!" she cried, and "Good for me!"), Ben nodded approvingly. "That's great, Birdy," he said, and she said, "Thanks, Benny." Rooting for each other may not be highlighted in the Miss Manners book, but it's definitely nice.

Then again, we endorse some unorthodox practices about politeness. I feel, for example, that when you plunk a steaming, buttered ear of it on your child's plate and he cries, "Ooooh—yum! Corn on the cob!" this is just as good as, if not better than, a plain old "Thank you." I also think that the pleasure of eating cold green salad with your fingers cannot be overestimated, and at home this is a perfectly acceptable dinnertime behavior. As is resting a comfortable bare knee against the edge of the table, the better to brace yourself while you tug enthusiastically at a sparerib with teeth and hands. (These are what we call the home-alone rules.)

I like explaining manners when kindness is the operative goal; I am inclined to think they're silly when it's not. Every now and then, though, there's a gray area—like the corn bread. "Why *is* it even gross?" Here at the dinner table, I'm thinking aloud now, repeating Ben's question back to him. "It's a good question, honey." "I mean," he says, "it's not gross on your plate. And then it's just chewed up, which is the same, but chewed." "That's true," I say, but already a lightbulb is illuminating the space above Ben's head. "I know!" he says. "It's closer to being poop than when it's on your plate! And the closer it is to being poop, the less polite it is." This is probably a fairly articulate rendering of another of society's basic tenets. Safe and Kind—and as far from turning to shit as possible. "Good thinking," I say. And Ben smiles at me and says, "Thank you."

II

ENDURING

How to Be Sick

Birdy's sick again. She awoke with a crusted-shut eye and staggered around like the blinded Oedipus until I went after her with a warm washcloth—and then she staggered around like a blinded, shrieking four-year-old harpy. Now we're at the doctor's office, where she's heartbreakingly quiet, her eye an oozing pink wink of its usual twinkle. When I bend to touch my lips to her skin, she whispers, "You're kissing my forehead but really you're taking my *fever*." She's a wily one, that Birdy, but she's nice and cool.

Our family has been tossing sickness back and forth like a hot potato, but one that wasn't actually hot enough, so now it's contaminated with salmonella and also many viruses. Ben, brushing his teeth just last night, stopped short with a hand on the water cup. "Wait," he said. "*Who's* got germs now?" "Well, you've got a sore throat, right?" I said, and he said, "That's true, but Birdy was barfing. Plus—doesn't she have a fever now?"

She didn't, but I scrubbed the cup with soap and water while Ben waited with a foaming mouthful of toothpaste. "It *shucks* to be *shick*," he said.

And Ben should know. In his seven-year lifetime, he and his sister have been diagnosed with, in alphabetical order: blocked tear ducts, bronchitis, the common cold, conjunctivitis, constipation, Coxsackie, croup, diarrhea, ear infections, eczema, enterovirus, fifth disease, hives, influenza, jaundice, Lyme disease, Norwalk virus, pneumonia, reactive airway disease, respiratory syncytial virus, roseola, rotavirus, sinusitis, staphylococcus, streptococcus, thrush, and tonsillitis. Our medicine cabinet is a museum of infection, curated through various displays of ointments, syrups, and chewable tablets. I can tell you the Latin name as well as the length of incubation, duration of contagion, route of infection (including my least favorite: fecal-oral), and preferred method of treatment for any particular illness. And our kids are, inarguably, blessed with good health.

For me, parenting sick children—even *healthy* sick children—has been trial by fire. Trial by towering inferno. "If I'd known it was going to be like this…" I said tearfully once, frantic with worry over Ben, newborn and coughing. "Oh, honey—you would have *what?*" Michael asked gently. "Not *had him?*" I let the question evaporate—it was rhetorical, of course, absurd—but I wondered. Ben coughed until he gagged on his own phlegm; his feverish feet were like miniature loaves of bread, hot out of the oven. Anxiety percolated so violently in me that I imagined it bursting through my skin, puffing out into the atmosphere like a toxic gas. Our baby book fell open to the pages on coughing, even though I had already committed them to memory. We squirted candy-colored medicine into that microscopic rosebud of a mouth, that mouth that had tasted nothing but milk, and it felt as natural and right as putting Tabasco in my own eye. We hadn't yet learned the fundamental lesson—kids get sick and then, god willing, *they get better again*—and so I fantasized about the baby dying because it was the only end I could see to my worry that he would die. I tell you this by way of confession.

It is not how I feel anymore. Although in the waiting room now, Birdy announces, "We don't play with the toys here," and this is true. I mean, really. The doctors will all tell you that most kids get sick from touching objects that germy kids have touched before them—but then, yes, let's set up a dollhouse right where all the sick and well kids are hanging out together! Let's play spin the bottle here in the waiting room. Let's have a taffy pull! It's like an episode of *Candid Camera* with gastroenteritis as its theme. One of the doctors even has a chain full of little animals hanging from his belt, and when he encourages Birdy to touch them I think, *Why don't you just spray her with impetigo?*

Did you read that article in *The New Yorker* a few years ago— the one about the way germs spread? Researchers took a guy with a common cold, injected him with some kind of dye, and sent him to a dinner party; at the end of the evening, they turned on a special fluorescent light to see how far his mucosal output (i.e., *snot*) had migrated. And what do you know? It was *everywhere:* on every doorknob and light switch, on every guest's hair, wineglass, and lips. I may be the only reader of that piece who wasn't surprised. Motherhood conferred on me a kind of germ ESP, as if that fluorescent light were somehow built into my very eyeballs. Plus, I'm a magnet for confession: if your child barfed out the car window on the way to the birthday party, she will end up climbing into my lap, kissing me on the lips, and telling me about it (and I will end up darting away to the bathroom to scrub my neck and kids with lye).

But now that childhood illness is a cloud more of immediate, practical proportions than epic, spiritual ones, I try to appreciate the tender silver lining of quiet time to spend together. (This tenderness is especially welcome, since many illnesses are preceded by a day of nagging—"Finish your bratwurst. And quit all that whining!"—before the child falls feverishly asleep over the Candy Land board.) Birdy climbs up into the cool expanse of our bed, and I bring her poached eggs and applesauce on a tray, feeling like a happy actor in a play about motherhood. I will get out the box of old holiday cards for her to sort, and then I will read her our favorite sick-day books— Patricia MacLachlan's *Sick Day*, Vera Rosenberry's *When Vera Was Sick*—and stroke her sweaty hair while she falls asleep. It's a scramble to figure out work schedules *(You take the morning off, and I'll come home early, okay?)* and dry all those extra loads of laundry while your child clings and regresses and wants to weep and be carried everywhere and have her back scratched and throw up in your hair. But the trick is not to be jaded. I try to remember how it felt when they were new and I longed to be the very muscle of their hearts so that I could be sure the blood would get pumped properly through their veins. I try to remember that there are parents everywhere, wheeling and dealing with god over their children's lives, for whom a garden-variety virus would be something like a gift. I try to remember that these snuffly little annoying children will leave us one day.

Now the doctor asks Birdy if her eye is sick, and she nods gravely, silent as a blade of grass. When the drops sting, she cries silently, whispers, "Pick me," which means "Pick me up." She says it again when we get home—"Pick me"—and I hold her on the couch, rock her gently like a baby, and like a baby she falls asleep in my arms. Her prizefighter eye is squinched shut and her round face is flushed, but her heart beats steadily against my bicep. *I do,* I think. *In sickness and in health, I pick you.*

How to Heal

It's nap time in the manger. The rosy, porcelain-skinned baby is sleeping quietly beside his mother, who dozes on her back on the barn floor, despite a broken-off right hand and the way her legs have been bent into ceramically permanent kneeling. There's not a soul awake in the stable: an ox snores softly between two kings; the shepherd lies down with the lamb; a camel slumbers beneath his ceramic saddle. It's like the aftermath of a weird frat party. Opium Day at the circus. "It's pretty crowded in there!" I say, and Birdy puts her finger to her lips and gently shushes me. "I love this *crush*," she whispers for the zillionth time, and for the zillionth time I whisper back, "I know."

A day earlier, the cashier at the Salvation Army wrapped each piece carefully in newspaper and said, with understated Slavic enthusiasm, "Good deal, crèche." Indeed. Ten barely chipped figures, shedding thatched stable included, for $3.99: in the thick of the holiday season, I was treating myself to a little bargain therapy. Or maybe I just wanted to watch Birdy play. We're accomplishing all our usual festivities: packaging home-made marshmallows for our neighbors, frying latkes, crack-ing walnuts by the woodstove while Frank Sinatra croons "Si-lent Night" scratchily from the record player. But the holiday warmth is like a thin sweater, and I'm cold beneath it.

We've moved—moved in the middle of an ice storm, with frozen branches clattering to the ground around us like bones—and our new house is ancient and drafty. I lie on the couch under a blanket and pine a bit for our cozy old too-small house that was always warm. Moving is hard, and the exhaustion is normal. But what about the sadness? We strung up the twinkling lights straightaway, lit the candle chimes and the menorah in the echoing emptiness of new rooms. We're just across town from where we were a week earlier, and noth-ing is wrong, not really. Everything is great, in fact. Except that Birdy has one of her endless winter bouts of bronchitis, and we sit up with her in the night, pull her into the dark of the strange bathroom to steam her in the strange shower, while she coughs and coughs her four-year-old lungs out. Come morn-ing, we paw tiredly through boxes to look for the teaspoons, to look for the peanut butter. Come afternoon, we forget to pick up Ben from school, and when I finally rush in from the bit-ter cold to find him in the principal's office, he says, near tears, "Where *were* you?" I don't know. Probably in the mouse-smell basement, studying the baffling new fuse box.

At night I lie in my husband's arms and cry. It's the anniversary of a miscarriage we had last year, and I cry for the baby we hadn't planned and had barely known about. I cry for that microscopic loss and the bigger one: here in this new house, we are not likely to become new parents again. "Birdy was born in the old house." I picture our daughter with her red newborn scalp, her fig-sized fists. "Well, not actually *in* the house," I admit. "But, you know, it's the house she came home to." Moving feels less like *moving on up* and more like *moving away*—away from the wooden windowsills pitted with evidence of teething, from the measuring wall with the comically low pencil marks, away from babies in the house, babies on the way, babies in our future. Now I'm weepy and flat-bellied in my lovely new house with my beautiful growing children. I am so glad and grateful, I am. But sometimes the orchestra plays something in swelling chords of luck and joy, and all I can hear is that one violin sawing out a thin melody of grief.

But then here's Birdy, kneeling to unwrap each piece of the crèche like the treasure that it is, lining everyone up on the coffee table with a million questions. As may be typical of agnostic half-Jews, I don't really know the whole story. "Those are the Magi," I say confidently. "The three wise men who brought gifts for the baby." "Then why are there five of them?" Birdy wants to know, and I shake my head, squint at the figures. "This one might be Joseph," I say. "The baby's stepfather. And maybe that's the shepherd whose stable they're sharing? I'm not actually sure." "What presents did they bring?" Birdy asks now, and when I answer with the mysterious "Frankincense and myrrh," she says, like the Nativity accountant she has become, "Mama, that's only *two* presents." Before I can respond, Birdy has already moved on. "Why are there farm animals *and* zoo animals?" she wants to know now. "And who's the baby's real dad?"

Jesus wakes briefly and the ox, maternal in his gently bovine way, gets up to cuddle him while snow drifts past our new windows, blankets our new garden beds, where, surely, beneath the ice, spring bulbs are dreaming of green. But now it's back to bed for everyone: wall-to-wall kings and shepherds, cows and camels and an exhausted mother whose happy-sad eyes never close. Birdy hums a little lullaby, kisses the tops of porcelain heads, man and beast each in turn, and peace washes over all of us. However much you might envy Mary her newborn, and whatever you believe or don't believe about Jesus Christ, there is just no getting around the beauty of this little girl tucking everyone in safely over and over again. It's all a kind of Christmas dollhouse to her, sure—but to me it's the timeless and universal concept of *shelter.* And so, finally, I am home.

How to Be Awake in the Dark

I'm realizing that I know a great deal about my weaknesses as a parent. Impatience, for example: the way I will flash you a tight-lipped smile and say, "I'm not really looking to spend all day in here," when you want to study the leaking nozzle of the soap dispenser in the gas-station bathroom. Distraction: the way I will glaze over while you imagine aloud a new board game *(Will the mozzarella keep better wrapped tightly in plastic wrap or covered with water? Will that tooth ever fall out or is it just going to hang there at a crazy angle forever? Do I look more like I'm listening or more like I'm staring at the crazy tooth?)* so that when you finally get to the part where you ask if the game should be called Sneak, Peek, and Lose Your Turn, or Money Drawers, I will say, "Ummmm," in that obvious, stalling way of distracted parents everywhere, and then I will say, "What about Peek in Your Drawers?" which at least makes you laugh. Fear: the way your memories of childhood will be dominated by my grimacing and saying "Careful!" and covering my eyes every time you walk near the top of the staircase or balance a spoon on your head.

But I'm good in the night. I'm actually even kind of *great* in the night: easy to wake, friendly, glad to see the children again when they stagger into our bedroom in the dark. Which is funny because (a) I am not always even totally happy to see them during the *day* ("Yeah, yeah, that's hilarious. *Poop right into your own poopy butt.* Very funny. Look, if you want to stay in the bath with me, can we talk about something else?") and (b) If you had told me three years ago that I was ever going to miss them in the night, I would have laughed the hysterical laughter of the sleep-deprived, then fallen, laughing, asleep at the table with my deranged forehead resting on my empty coffee cup.

But now the sound of their little feet in the hallway floods me with happiness. Tonight I hear the feet approaching, and then retreating, and then approaching again, which means Birdy, who always gets halfway before turning back for Ruthie Doll or Pansy Chimpanzee, or whomever she has left mistakenly behind in bed. And then there she is with the dolly clutched under her arm, clambering warmly in beside me. She has a stomachache, she tells me cheerfully, but her eyes are so big and shiny and smiley in the moonlight that I do not even lurch up to shove a wastebasket under her chin. "What about some crackers?" I wonder, and she thinks yes, that would probably do the trick.

Lately Birdy's been coughing again. Again or still? Whichever. On and on. Her cheeks are so surreally pink that she looks like a cheap-doll version of herself. Her chest rattles. Or she gets a new virus on top of the old coughing. Like the night she raises a sleeping hand to brush the hair out of her face, and I see that the hand she raises is shaking. When I sneak a thermometer under her armpit, she yells, "Who is that?" without waking up, then mutters something that sounds like a muffled string of obscenities—"Rassum brassum," like Muttley in that old cartoon. Her armpit temperature is 103, which I translate first, tiredly, as 102 and then, correctly, as 104.

"Should I wake her up and give her something?" I ask Michael, and he says, "I don't know." We trade these exact lines back and forth all night, like we're rehearsing a surrealist play about actors rehearsing a play about a sick child. "We should probably just let her sleep," he offers, and I agree.

Every time Birdy coughs, my stomach clenches. My whole body clenches. There's a rhythm to it: In, out, *cough cough cough*. In, out, *cough cough cough*. Now that it's the light of day, I can live with the clenching. In the night it makes me feel like my skin is going to split open and I will be reborn as a lizard to slither away into the trees. I think some about earplugs, which I want but know I would never use. That's part of our job as parents, isn't it? Not to turn away from our children's pain, whatever its cause or expression. To stay as fully present as we possibly can. Over and over, I put my palm on her hot, mumbling body and do the thing that, if you didn't know me better, you would probably think was prayer.

But this night, now, Birdy doesn't cough, and I think to be grateful for the not-coughing. She just lies propped up beside me, munching noisily on Saltines, slurping noisily from her water bottle, and conversing in her deafening whisper while her father dreams peacefully beside us (bless him / damn him). It's like a really good date, but in another country, with a person who thinks that shouting will help you better understand their native Portuguese. "Mom?" she says, when she finishes her snack. "Mom? Mom? Did you think I was going to eat, like, *cracker cracker cracker, water?* Or like I did do, which is *cracker, water, cracker, water, cracker, water?*" "Mom?" she says. "Mom? Is that grapy stuff that made my cheeks so shiny—is it lip *blass* or lip *glass?*

"Or lip *bloss?*"

There's nothing else I'm supposed to be doing, no distractions. Just me and this Birdy girl, who nods when I ask if I can turn out the light now, curls into a ball beside me, plunges her hand down the front of my shirt, and sleeps, her dark-lashed peach of a face the dearest thing I've ever had the good sense to notice.

How to Attend an Absurdist Tea Party

It's one of those long, lit-up spring evenings: daffodils blooming, the bleeding hearts just emerging, the world an ache of blue and green. Could there be a better moment to spill an entire pitcher of iced peppermint tea from the coffee table? Of course not! We're eating our pizza in the living room near the open windows, and Birdy insists on refilling her own glass. First there's just a single misplaced drip, only then she's distracted by the drip, loses her grip, and drops the pitcher, knocking over her own glass in the process and sending a wave of tea over the side of the table and onto the (idiotically) white rug. Also into the open storage compartments of the table, where the baskets of books, games, and magazines become immediately flooded.

In someone else's normal life—I am imagining here—people laugh, scramble after sponges, tacitly agree to resume their conversations in a minute or two, once all the *Your Big Backyards* have been mopped off, the puzzles set out to dry, plates rinsed and refilled. But instead I leap up to get a dish towel while my children proceed with dinner like pediatric robots who have been programmed to stay on task. *Must keep eating. Must keep talking.* "I need a new piece of pizza," Birdy says, poking at her crust, which is now soaking under the half-inch of tea in her plate. "Another artichoke piece. Cut it with scissors again that exact same way in the exact same number of pieces so I can eat it littlest to biggest." It's like one reel of film superimposed onto another: the frantic sodden crisis blurred into the chatty perseverance.

Despite the dish towel, tea is still pouring off the table's edge, and I'm trying to catch it in a cup, blotting at the sodden rug with a useless paper napkin. "Honey, can you please get me a dry dish towel?" I say to Ben, only he doesn't hear me because *he's still talking.* "Clara in chorus? She was the only alto singing the high part? And all the other altos were like, 'I am *so* not singing the high part.' And I was like, to myself, 'I'd sing the high part!' But then I remembered that I already *do* sing the high part!" I love his new Valley Girl way of talking, and there may be no more comical understatement in the world than describing Ben as a soprano. But still. Now is not the time. "Honey," I say, and he says, "Oh, right! Dish towel!" and leaps up obligingly, *still talking.* "It was Smarties day? For having all your right music and a pencil? But I so totally had the wrong pencil! I mean, I had, like, a *Halloween* stub of a pencil, and the teacher didn't even care and I got a roll of Smarties anyway!"

"Honey?" I say, and Ben says, consolingly, *"No te preocupes,* Mama," and returns with the dish towel. "Well, Ben?" This is

Birdy again, with her classic combative opener. "Ben, it's *oy estoy moy ucapata.*" "Okay, Birdy," he says, and she says, "It *is.*" "Okay, Birdy, fine," he says again, and she scowls at him. Ben is helping me with the tea now, dabbing with the dish towel, but all I can picture for some reason is me with my head lopped off, blood spurting like a geyser from my neck stump, while the children bicker and talk and chew their food.

And actually what I'm remembering is how Ben used to fall asleep in the car when Birdy cried. On spring nights just like this one. She'd be screaming her small red face off, with that terrycloth neck-support horseshoe wedged around her furious head, her mouth a wild, toothless hollow of misery, and Ben would keep talking in a normal conversational pitch — "I just…because the oranges…the horse pooping…didn't think it would!" — and I couldn't even hear him for the screaming (Birdy's) and the panic (mine). And then suddenly, as if the baby were crooning a delicate lullaby, Ben's eyes would flutter and close, and the two of them would be behind me, yelling and sleeping, like some bizarre yin-yang introduction to parenthood.

Four years later, life still turns crazy on a dime. I can't always tell with Birdy what the deal is with talking. I mean, if you transcribed a typical conversational day at our house, perhaps it would look on paper as if everyone spoke an equal and regular amount. Perhaps only if you italicized all of Birdy's loudness would you understand that this person I share my house with sees the world through a rose-colored megaphone.

"Onions have a kind of a *papery* skin!" is the first thing she might say upon waking, for instance. But italics really don't do justice to the groggy shouting of this observation into my face. Birdy tends to be lying on top of me, so she'll rear her head back to say it again: "A *papery* skin! And you *shred* it off—you just kind of *SHRED* it off, right, Mama? You *SHRED* it."

It is craziest when Birdy's half asleep, a dozy time one might incorrectly associate with whispers and quiet musing. Like the night she wanders into our bedroom, sputtering with woe because one of her leg Band-Aids has fallen off in the bed. After a fresh one is obtained and applied, she sneaks exuberantly into bed between Michael and me—like the physical equivalent of a stage whisper—and seems to sleep while we parents discuss her weepy, spreading rash. Her eyes snap open. "WHAT'S OLD NAVY?" Her mouth is a bellows, words pushed out in roaring blasts. She's like one of those friendly cartoon dragons who just want to say hello but end up setting your braids on fire. "Old Navy is that store with that truck and the pretend dog and the rubber ball machine," I say, "where we get sun hats and flip-flops." "I thought so." Her eyes close again. Can you put hydrocortisone on a child? We don't know. We've heard that very hot water is helpful. The eyes snap open again. "HOW DID IT HURT MY LEG?" *What?* "WHY DID OLD NAVY GIVE ME A RASH?" "Oh, honey. No. Not Old Navy. *Poison ivy.* That plant when we were looking at the lilacs. Remember?" "Oh. Poison ivy." Her eyes close again, then snap open before Michael and I have even stopped laughing. "Wait, wait," she says. "Tell me again. HOW did Old Navy make ALL THESE SPOTS ON MY LEG?"

My mother and I were recently pulling weeds out of her asparagus bed, the kids chattering in the background while they pushed seeds into the ground. My mom had sighed and said, "I never tire of those little voices," and I'd agreed with absentminded sentimentality, "Me either." And then a second later: "Wait—what am I saying? I tire of them *constantly*." And my mom had laughed because there was Birdy already, her face pressed right up against mine, saying, "Mom. Mom. Mom. Mom. I have a toenail that's a bit GRUBBY." "Ah," I had said. "Some toenails are like that." "Mom. Mom. Mom. Mom. I have a toenail that's a bit SHAGGY." Whenever I try to remind her about saying "Mom" one time and then giving me a moment to respond, she says, like a stand-up comedian, "Mama? Mama? Mama? I FORGOT."

Sometimes I worry that Birdy talks so loud and stammeringly because I've been distracted. I don't know quite how to describe this distraction, except to say that I'll vow to pay attention to one of the children's stories, and then I'll remember to rouse myself only when the conclusion—"AND IT WAS INSIDE MY SOCK THE WHOLE ENTIRE TIME!"—detonates through the fog of my atmosphere. I'll have to shake my head and say, "I'm sorry, honey. Tell me that last part one more time." What is it with my inattention? Technology? Middle age? Mercury poisoning from my fillings? Or is it simply the fact that the kids' stories are like those telethons from childhood, where you flip the TV off and eat your franks and beans and take a bath and go to sleep and wake up and eat your Buc Wheats cereal and turn the TV back on—and Jerry Lewis is *still talking.* I just don't want to become one of those parents—one of those *dads,* to be precise—with the kids tugging on the hem of their suit coats, the kind that need to learn a Big Lesson in a movie with grief at its core. I want to kneel down lower and listen harder. Even as my braids go up in flames.

How to Be Wrong

Over our bowls of white bean soup, Ben is talking happily about the playdate he's just returned from. In the course of this happy talking, he describes some of the things that he and his friends were daring one another to do: write swear words in a notebook ("Like *stupid,* and other even worse ones! Actually, no, that was the worst one"), draw on their arms with a marker, jump off the bed. Hooligans! I love this branching out into the fullness of childhood. It's the era of secrets and mild daring that I once feared Ben might never enter, stuck as he was for years and years to my hip and rib cage. But later, as he's dealing out cards for a quick before-bed game, it occurs to me to lecture him.

"You guys are great—it's great that you're having so much fun," I begin, with smug magnanimity, because I'm not like those other parents who want their children eternally sweeping cinders from the hearth and memorizing flash cards on particle physics. I want them to be having fun! Sort of. "But I just want to be sure you always remember to do things because you want to, and not because other people are making you feel like you should." And Ben interrupts me to say, "Yeah, yeah, yeah. I know. I know. Are these cards shuffled?"

Maybe this is a whisper from the future about the challenge of raising a teenager: the way the blowing off of one's guidance can trigger an almost hormonal need to ratchet up the tone and volume of a lecture. Because I ratchet it up. I don't think it helps that Ben's current conversational mode seems to be *Talk to the curtain of hair.* We ask that he wear his long hair pulled out of his face for school, but at home it often seems to function as a hirsute soundproofing mechanism. And so I preach on about peer pressure and safety while Ben and his hair rearrange the cards in their hand and beat me at Crazy Eights and say, "Mm-hmm. I understand. I know. Okay."

I grow sullen. Quiet, cool. My ugliest, neediest self. What do I want? For Ben to look up and say, "You're so right, Mama. I am illuminated by your wise counsel and only sorry not to have communicated my deep gratitude more thoughtfully." I don't know. Because when I finally say, belaboringly, "I feel like you weren't really listening to me," and he says, "Sorry. Sorry, Mama. Sorry," I feel like the frightening, impotent Wizard of Oz, but played by Joan Crawford.

This gentle boy. Honestly. He is such a tender-heart. Earlier he'd said, in the voice of the little stuffed beaver he was holding, "Oooh, I'm too chilly! I need cuddles." And then his eyes had filled with tears. "Oh, no, did you make yourself cry?" I'd asked, and he'd nodded and smiled. Human infants—forget it. You could drop a baby on its head right next to him, and he'd carry on with his finger knitting, humming "Yankee Doodle Dandy" while it screamed; he'd sooner soak a doll with kerosene, set it to blazes, and swallow the ashes than kiss its rubbery cheek. But animals! He once choked up and said *"Don't!"* to me because I had nuzzled a miniature stegosaurus's nose against his neck and complained, in its croaky old voice, "Benny, I'm *extinct!"* I don't really think this kid needs reminding that I'm the boss of him.

The parent I want to be floats in and out of my life, and some days it speaks through me, and other days I lunge after it like it's a shaft of sunlight I want to capture. Last night I regaled the kids with a memory of the X-ray glasses I fantasized about ordering from the back of an *Archie* comic, only then a friend of mine actually got a pair and there were just skeletons painted on the lenses. "I thought I was going to be able to see through people's clothes," I explained, and Ben's face lit up. "I *always* want to see people naked!" he practically shouted. "I thought that was just me!" And when Michael and I laughed and explained that this was, in fact, *everybody*—that kids and grown-ups alike share this goggle-eyed interest in nudity—Ben was thrilled. It felt like such an easy gift to give him. Under the wrappings and the ribbons, the simple message: "You're fine. You're perfect!" And tonight, I don't know. Tonight it's coal in his stocking. It's "What's wrong with you?" even though those words are never, of course, spoken. It's bullying him to warn him about bullying. "Don't let people intimidate you.

DID YOU HEAR WHAT I SAID?" We can shore our children up, be their emotional sandbags, scaffold the heights of their confidence. Or, terribly, not.

I know better. I've read some of the actual scientific research that suggests that kindness leads to heightened creativity, better thinking and problem solving, greater energy, and stronger motivation. In short, to happiness. It should be the easiest thing in the world, the most natural. But, then, our worries about the future can make us corrupt the present where our kids are actually living now. *I have to make you unhappy now so someone else won't make you unhappy later!* It's the parenting version of taking a sledgehammer to your own car so you won't have to worry about vandals. And so you can feel the weight of the tool in your hand. When I apologize to Ben in his bed, wrapping my arms around his littleness and striped pajamas, he shakes his head, doesn't know what I'm talking about. So, okay. Enough already—it's already been about me all along tonight. I kiss his cheeks and let it go.

III

LEARNING

How to Be Raised by Animals

Because I am so choked by work that I practically need someone to stab a pen into my neck for breathing through, I put on a movie for the kids. I set them up to watch *The Jungle Book* through dinnertime: the thing we call Pizza Movie Night even though tonight's "pizza" is Trader Joe's spanakopita. It's a brilliant idea, eating spanakopita in bed! Because phyllo pastry is just so interesting, the way it shatters into a fountain of flakes when you so much as look at it. By the end of the movie, we're covered in pastry like it is ashes and we're victims at Pompeii, fossilized with our spinach filling. Later, I will munch absently on the crumbs while reading in bed, until I put something in my mouth that turns out to be not actually spanakopita.

For now, though, I'm just sitting with my laptop, keeping the kids company, but only half watching. I couldn't resist this old movie, especially since it was on the sale rack at the Salvation Army for fifty cents. I have a vague uneasiness about the film's racist undertones (aren't there *monkeys* singing "I Wanna Be Like You," but in conspicuously African-American Louis Armstrong voices?) and a similarly vague attraction to its old-fashioned pacing, but I'm not paying enough attention to confirm either. In fact, when the kids ask me questions, I can't answer them. "Is he a good guy or a bad guy?" they want to know, and I squint at the screen, see a hugely coiled, sneaky-eyed python, and guess, like a dim psychic, "Bad guy?" Whenever the children crack up, I glance at the screen to see the bear rubbing his butt crack on a tree or Mowgli bumping into an elephant's butt crack. I should have *butt crack* tattooed across my own forehead just to guarantee their permanent joie de vivre.

I look up to see a shapely, cat-eyed girl filling up her water jar, then look up again a minute later to see the credits rolling. "Was that a happy ending?" the children wonder, and I say truthfully, "I really don't know. What do you think?" "If I'd been raised by animals, it would be sad to leave them," Ben says. "What's that word? Semisweet?" "Bittersweet," I say. "Me too," Birdy says. "I would stay with the animals." When I was their age—eight and five—I would have chosen the same. I practically would even now.

Next the children want to know if it ever happens in real life, and I tell them the real-life story of Romulus and Remus being nursed by a wolf. Okay, I do explain that it's actually a myth, but we decide to look it up on Wikipedia, and all I can say— as I say so often about the Internet—is "Who knew?" I mean, really. The entry on the Rome-founding twins sends you to an entry on "feral children" that is longer than my own personal dangling teats, with which I could suckle Romulus and Remus from two counties away. I read aloud, and it's never clear which stories are to be taken as myths and which, if any, are factual. It all blurs together into sentences like "Most feral children prefer to eat off the floor," as if you were asking for advice about what to do if one shows up at your next holiday party. There are lists of famous feral children and their adoptive animal families: lots of dogs and wolves, bears and monkeys, even gazelles and the occasional farm animal (Daniel the Andes Goat Boy, as well as the Bamberg Boy, raised by cattle). I consider a cow for a parent: great milk, lax discipline. You half expect to see babies raised by fruit bats and armadillos, by earthworms and badgers. Against my better judgment, we follow a link to something like feralchildren.com. Maybe we could get a subscription to *Feral Child Fancier*, I think, because I'm hilarious like that—except then the site is actually sad. Less singing families of cartoon hedgehogs than frank abandonment.

And I should have been more careful. Later, half into her pajamas, Birdy is chewing her lip, her eyebrows pulled into a little *w* for *worried*. "So," she says, real casual-like. "Do you think your parents just, like, drop you off in the woods after they find the right kind of animal?" Ah. I explain that no, these are really unusual circumstances—probably not even real—where babies ended up in the woods or in the care of animals. I am careful not to use the words *lost* or *left*. And I'm surprised to realize that, in a Venn diagram, this conversation would actually overlap with ones we've had about adoption: reassurance that children are wanted and cared for, unease around the issue of how babies are parted from their birth parents in the first place. I'm not having the conversation I thought I was having, and I wonder what it would feel like if Birdy were adopted—whether I would think to say different kinds of things. Either way, this is a girl who needs reassurance. We are no longer talking about cartoons and friendly singing bears and how fun it would be to be raised by animals.

"We would never leave you," I tell her, and she makes a dismissive sound like "Pfff" and says, "I know *that!*" But her shoulders drop back down, and she leans happily against me. I am a bear, a wolf: I would protect her with my claws and teeth, slice open my own fur skin and wrap her in it if I had to, wrap her in this fierce, animal love.

How to See the Light Behind the Trees

We are skipping down the steep hill from the bathroom, Birdy and I, in the piney twilight of the campground. We've been coming here since before she was born, since the day she was conceived, in fact, when her father and I had loitered at home sexually, waiting for the rain to stop before finally driving to the campground. She and I have probably made this exact trip to and from this exact bathroom, oh, three hundred or so times. It is one of the few aspects of camping in which the beauty of the moment is not immediately apparent—what with holding my breath against the reeking dampness while greenhead flies buzz against the fluorescent light fixture and the daddy long-legs congregate in leggy tangles like Halloween props and I swat mosquitoes away from Birdy's hair while her pants pool around her ankles onto the wet cement floor and she hums and chats and unspools some toilet paper, spools it back up, and then decides, nope, not this time, maybe she'll try again later.

Oh, but cheer bubbles out of her, even here. Water sprays sideways out of the faucet, drenching her sleeves and shirtfront, and she peers into the sink and wonders aloud about the blue ring. While I explain about the copper oxidizing in the drain, she stands on tiptoe, craning to see herself in the mirror, where she stretches her face briefly into a version of *The Scream,* then says, "I don't really understand that, about the drain," and skips back outside through the beetle-encrusted screen door.

We pass the campsite where some kind of raucous family reunion is taking place: there are dozens of people, a cluster of enormous tents, multiple Coleman stoves sizzling out endless rounds of hot dogs and hamburgers, pancakes and bacon. "Is my latte ready yet?" I call out, as I do every time we pass, and they laugh. A large group of them is always playing beanbag toss, kids and grown-ups lined up in hooting, riotous teams. They are never not playing. "I picture one of them getting hurt," Ben said earlier. "And the rest of them all playing beanbag toss in the ER." There is also much loud playing of much loud rock music. "It must be fun to party all night long," Birdy sighs, like maybe she's Eddie Van Halen.

But now it's just this girl and me alone on the road, in the deepening dark, with the trees exhaling their clean smell all around us. This road! At two, Ben learned about looking both ways on this road, at three he crossed it proudly to fill his water bottle from the spigot, at six he and a friend walked alone up to the stone shelter to watch the sunset, and, yesterday, he had his very first head-over-heels bicycle wipeout right here, almost exactly where we're standing. He got up, brushed off his bruised ribs, his scraped knees, and hopped back on, pedaled away while I stood motionless with my heart in my stomach.

And this girl, my little one, with the s'more residue smudged across her forehead and into her bangs, with the constellation of bug bites sprayed across her cheeks—she ran up this road holding my hand, years ago, newly diaperless and in a big rush. Before then, I walked this road, humming, with her in the sling, Birdy with the big eyes, too excited about the waves and the hermit crabs and the Popsicle and the fire to let her poor tired self nap. I walked this road the summer she was sick, the summer I said to Michael, "Could she be this hot just from the sun?" And no, she couldn't be. I lay with her in the tent, willing her to cool down while we listened to the big kids splash in the pond below, and she smiled and smiled at me, kicking her fat, feverish, happy little legs.

I used to picture time as a rope you followed along, hand over hand, into the distance, but it's nothing like that. It moves outward but holds everything that's come before. Cut me open and I'm a tree trunk, rings of nostalgia radiating inward. All the years are nested inside me like I'm my own personal one-woman matryoshka doll. I guess that's true for everybody, but then I drive everybody crazy with my nostalgia and happiness. I am *bittersweet* personified.

Mostly, it just gets better and better: everybody swimming and biking and wiping their own cracks, fewer marshmallows stuck to weeping heads of hair, and less vigilance required from the grown-ups. I have always loved the camping, but now I look back and feel like maybe it kind of used to suck. I mean, there was the beach: nursing a hot and sandy somebody in a little blowing-away tent, a pee-bloated swim diaper soaking in my lap. Or the campsite itself, where I seemed to spend every minute chasing my miniature humans away from the road. I know I loved it. I did. But seriously.

Just recently, we watched a couple out by the bay with what was maybe a two-month-old. They were trying to keep it out of the sun, and the baby was red and crying, and the parents were taking turns wading into the water up to their ankles before darting back to make sure the other person wasn't mad at them for being gone so long, and I wanted to say, "Oh, go home. Turn on the AC and the TV, and just relax. You can go to the beach later, when it's older." But I remember how much fun we thought we were having—and were, I'm sure—and I spare them my demented advice.

But some things don't change at all. When I walk down this road with Birdy's hand in mine, it is this same moment from my entire life of mothering her: her curiosity. Her absolute hereness. "Is it true, about stars, about how we see them even if they're maybe not still shining?" she wants to know, and I could burst into tears, like the weirdo I am. "I think it is," I say, "but it is so hard to understand." I feel her fingers in mine, the full moon rising up into the pines like a cosmic lantern, the squirrels chuckling to themselves in the branches above us, and I want only *now*. The glow that lasts beyond itself.

The frogs have started up, honking to one another in the dark like an orchestra of kazoos, and Birdy stops walking to squint at something. "What *is* that," she asks, *"windows?"* I look where she's pointing, and what it is, is the last of the light over the pond, glowing through the trees, illuminating the spaces between them into flickering squares of blue. And what it's like is not anything, it's just this, the dark and the light and her small hand in mine, her sun-streaked braids, her trust. "Keep holding my hand," she says. "I'm closing my eyes." And I will, my Birdy love. I do.

How to Talk About Sex

When I was writing something, once, about talking to kids about sex, I read a book by an expert who warned parents not to misrepresent the facts. "Do not make up stories involving storks or other magical events," she advises—wise counsel, sure, but curious, given that just a few pages earlier she herself has shared this bit of magical gynecological thinking: "The baby will come out of the mother's vagina, which is very, very stretchy. It stretches wide enough for the baby to come out *and then goes back to the way it was before.*" Sure it does! Right after fairies break the evil spell that turned her vagina into an echoing warehouse! Or maybe in *heaven*.

It's not that you'd really want to tell your child the whole truth here (the baby will come out of the mother's vagina, which is very, very stretchy like an old tube sock with the disintegrating elastic, and later when the father sticks his foot back in, well, remember that time we ran out of buns, and you tried wrapping your hot dog in a tortilla?). Or a beautiful fairy tale (then the stork brings the mother a *new* vagina, just like her stretchy old one!). It's that talking to kids about sex seems to involve a peculiar mix of facts and euphemisms.

Needless to say, the alleged stretchiness of the vagina does not goad—or especially interest—eight-year-old Ben, who describes one of the library's where-did-I-come-from books as "very helpful" when we're done reading it. We've checked out a big stack to address his growing interest in bodies and sex— or if not sex, exactly, then something like *nakedness.* "But," he's saying shyly now, "the book actually leaves out that other part—the part I'm most interested in."

Indeed.

I'd wondered if the absence of actual intercourse was going to be noted. Most of the books just seem to load children into a kind of informational station wagon and drive them along various anatomical roadways, chatting sensibly and comfortably about penis and vagina, ovaries and testicles—and then, *zoing,* it catapults them across the canyon of sex, and the kids find themselves back in the car on the other side, chatting about uterus and baby without ever really having gotten a good look at the view.

This is not Ben's first encounter with intercourse or its absence. We were recently reading one of the kids' favorites, *How Was I Born?,* a Swedish book full of those brilliant fetus-in-outer-space photographs taken in utero, and one that offers two parallel stories: the human child's narrative about expecting a new baby brother, and the human-science narrative about embryology. When the kids were littler, we'd gotten in the habit of following only the cozy, subtler text, but now Ben was reading over my shoulder. "Hey, can you tell us that other part?" he said, and I was glad to. Only suddenly, on the very same page with the nice, comforting story ("My mom is called Sally. She's happy and sometimes wears glasses"), I choked on this little bone: "This means that the father puts his penis inside the mother's vagina and many sperm come out through his penis." This *same* father we've known for years? The beloved Daddy-called-Pete with the nice-smelling sweater? When I got to the end of the page, I turned bravely to Ben and said, "Wow. That's probably new information for you. Do you have any questions about it?" His eyeballs were practically rolling around in their sockets, but my son shook his head and said, "No." And then he clarified: "I mean, I've got, like, a *million* questions about it? But none that I even know how to ask."

And maybe that's sex in a nutshell. *A million questions that you don't know how to ask.* For kids, it's simultaneously everywhere and nowhere—like cockroaches that disappear when you flip the light on, and all you get is a strong impression of scurrying. It must seem so random to them. Now we're talking together solemnly about your penis and what it can do; now you're in trouble for talking about it at the dinner table; now it dangles down; now it sticks straight out; now we're discussing babies; and now, it seems, we're discussing lawn care or maybe chickens. The metaphors are more confusing than clarifying. Birdy once said, "So, wait—the daddy's seed plants on the mommy's egg?" And I pictured the way we'd once planted seeds in a hollowed-out eggshell filled with dirt; I pictured Birdy picturing that this was how babies got made: the drawn-on smiley face, grass growing in for hair, Mommy and Daddy in their clothes in the kitchen, shoveling dirt with a teaspoon.

When I sift through the facts gleaned from my own childhood, it's the mental equivalent of rows and rows of tidy files (multiplication tables, uppercase cursive, how to build an igloo) and then a black plastic trash bag full of sexual odds and ends. I learned the mystifying punch line "That's not my belly button either!" which made me laugh uncomprehendingly. I flipped through the 1975 Sears catalog in which—*Eureka!*—a model's penis peeked out below the hem of his boxer shorts. I was required to wear cotton underwear so that my vagina could "breathe" (years later, when I first heard of *The Vagina Monologues*, I imagined other people's crotches enunciating clearly while mine gasped and wheezed). I glimpsed various thatches of pubic hair after my swim lessons at the YMCA, where there was also a mysterious Tampax machine dispensing something that was definitely not candy. In the middle of *M*A*S*H* reruns, there were TV commercials for the naked glam-rock musical *Caligula*. My brother and I pressed our small, excited faces to the lake-house window to watch our uncle's bosomy first wife skinny-dip at dawn. I read Judy Blume's *Forever...*, which ruined the name Ralph for me—*forever*. And then there was the general blur of assorted hydraulic images: prongs and plugs, pumping pistons, levers and slots, everything pouring in and out like the human body was maybe just one big, slippery slot machine.

For all of my unsqueamish compulsion to talk frankly with Ben and Birdy, I'm starting to suspect that it's the same old trash bag for them, just different contents: the menstrual flotsam and jetsam that wash up monthly in our bathroom trash ("So the string just kind of hangs out your *butt?*"); the camels we saw humping noisily at the zoo ("Awkward!"); the fact that, since the children were born, their father and I have been doing it *nonstop* (Ha ha ha! Zzzzz); the dirty pranks Ben noticed in a shop where he was checking out a gag plastic cat turd ("I don't get it. It looks like a present, but then it's empty and it has a hole and it says... *dick in a box?* Weird. But this is cute! It's a little drawing board for making pictures of beavers! Oh wait... ew. What *is* that?"); Birdy "hatching" her doll babies by jumping up and down until they fall out the bottom of her shirt (dream on, sweet girl).

Nonetheless, it was only when Ben overheard me talking to Michael about an inadvertently pregnant straight friend ("Considering they weren't actually trying, she sounds pretty excited!") that I realized how much we'd left out. "How could you get pregnant if you weren't trying to?" he asked, genuinely baffled. "I mean, that makes no sense. You only do the thing to get pregnant so you can make a baby, right?" I can gab the day away about making babies—but *sex for pleasure?* This conversation turns out to be as natural as sawing off my own foot. "Not always," I said, in my Talking to Children About Sex voice, which is paranormally loud and calm. "That thing grown-ups do to make a baby—it actually feels good to them, so sometimes they do it anyway." Notice I am speaking in the third person here, like the coward I am. Even so, Ben's face? It was as if he'd played the cat-turd prank on his own self.

Now I stop to think before responding to Ben about "that other part"—the one he's "most interested in." I recall the advice of a psychologist friend who once cautioned me not to assume that you understand what your children are asking, reminding me of that old joke where the kid asks, "Where did I come from?" and after the parents finish their big, long story about ovulating and ejaculation, the kid says, "No, I mean was it Cleveland or St. Louis?" And so I ask, "What other part, honey?" And Ben answers, laughing, "The *booty!*" Of course. "Um, honey? Tell me what part you think your bottom plays in making babies." Ben laughs again and says, "Oh, right! I guess the booty is more like bathroom talk. I'm just curious about it, is all." My children's understanding of reproduction seems to overlap with fart jokes—even though it's more a vague blur than any precise kind of misunderstanding.

And maybe it's all a vague blur anyway. Our job is to offer the facts of life as clearly as possible—and then, well, maybe we've got to let the mystery be. Part of what makes human sexuality special *is* the unspeakableness of it, of longing and pleasure and the way bodies intertwine with love. The absurdity too: not just the erections springing up all across your eighth-grade math class, but the way it's amazing and hilarious and weird and transcendent all at once.

Like now. The kids are drawing from an Ed Emberley book called *Make a World*. "Ed Emberley should do a *Make a Penis* book," Ben chuckles. "I mean, that's pretty much what kids

want to know how to draw, all the holes and cracks and stuff."
"Make a penis!" Birdy echoes, adding the predictable "Make a booty!" and hee-hawing until she wheezes. The kids are dying laughing ("Make a penis! Make a booty!"). These kids, who started life as desire, friction, cells dividing, a flutter of movement. Whom we love more than life itself.

How to Evolve

Now I'm talking to the kids about the Galápagos Islands because it's Darwin's birthday. "No it's not," Michael interjects. "It's the hundred and fiftieth anniversary of the publication of *On the Origin of Species*." Whatever. I am in love with evolution, but what exactly happened out at the Galápagos I'm less clear about. I attend to ideas in passionate—if brief—flurries of attention. I can be aghast over a headline I've misinterpreted in a newspaper story I haven't actually read. "They're replacing school nurses with robots!" I might cry, indignant, and Michael will say, "I think that's just an article about stuff MIT graduate students are inventing." Oh.

"Distraction is adaptive," I explain to the children. "If I did only one thing at a time, your lunch boxes would be packed every day with air and then you'd never survive to reproduce, now, would you?"

No. They would not. Do you remember how natural selection works? No, not the smooth and wrinkled peas; that was genetics. Keep sifting through your high school educational debris. It's the other thing, the pale peppered moths on dark trees getting picked off by the birds. Remember? Or has "survival of the fittest" kind of blurred into "Manifest Destiny," and now it gives you a bad white-people-giving-away-free!-smallpox-blankets feeling to recall it? It's not like that. Nor does survival of the fittest really have a *fitness* component—it doesn't mean that your daughter's ropy and muscled karate instructor will thrive to birth a million babies like a sea turtle while you, with your giant corduroy thighs rubbing together with a *shkrrr-shkrrr* sound, will drop immediately dead. It's about whether particular traits help a particular organism live long enough to produce offspring, a phenomenon called reproductive success. Your husband could do you from behind while you were bent over to sort the Tupperware drawer. And if you got pregnant and passed along your organizational skills to your offspring? Evolutionary *bingo!* Reproductive success.

For now, the kids and I stick to our conversations about various visible traits and how they might be adaptive. Let me say this: if you live in the world as a student of natural selection, you will never be bored. The children study the eyes of animals to determine if they're predators or prey. Prey have those nervous side eyes, usually with the big nervous ears, twitching and swiveling around to see who's coming to eat them and from where; picture a bunny, a mouse, Bambi's dead mother. Predators' eyes stare out from the front of their heads. "The better to chase you with, my dear," nine-year-old Ben says in his best

Big Bad Wolf voice, even though we humans are predators too (except for maybe your one cousin with the nervous side eyes whom you felt a strange urge to chase).

We stroke our pussycat and analyze him for adaptivity. Fur to keep him warm, of course, whiskers to avoid bumping into nighttime doorways, and what about purring? We don't know. "It makes you want to take care of him," Ben hypothesizes, which is so totally true. I picture the kittens turning on their irresistible little motors, the mother cat thinking, "Oh, *fine*," and rolling over to expose her rows of exhausted teats. I picture my babies smiling up at me at the exact moment I was contemplating how to discreetly rid myself of them. I picture myself weeping instead, spilling over with love, and yoinking a milky boob from my nightgown. They've actually studied this—the way babies' smiles trigger massive hits of dopamine and oxytocin in their parents, biological and adoptive both. Babies are a pretty good high.

"Being cute is adaptive," six-year-old Birdy says, as if reading my mind. She's thinking still about the pussycat, but I'm thinking about her: the big eyes, the helpless littleness, the wobbly dependence.

I kiss her plummy cheeks and say, "It is."

"So is being beautiful," Ben says, hair falling around his face like dark silk, his lips the color of berries. "Like the male hummingbirds." We watched one at the feeder all summer: a head sleeked over with emerald feathers, the neck banded in iridescence. I'm sure the girls were going crazy. I picture the scarlet cardinal seducing his fawn-colored mate, male peacocks fanning the riot of their tails, the hot crimson wattles of a cock.

Sex is a big part of it, the pleasure-rigged engineering that keeps the species from extinction, all the stinky snatches of body hair like so much pheromonal quicksand, the blood rushing hither and yon in its tumescent quest for continuity. "Enjoy it," I like to tease Michael. "I'm going to be done with this after menopause." If it were adaptive for us to have sex for our entire lives, would everything really dry up like that at a certain point? Viagra is hardly an adaptive invention, everyone's grandpa running around with a four-hour woody.

Of course evolutionary arguments aren't just grand, analytical riddles. They also get mustered to justify various patterns of domination: women should suckle everybody; gay people should concede the barren hydraulics of their coupling; pregnancy should end in birth. If someone's doing something you don't like, just go ahead and say that it's unnatural and non-adaptive, even if you claim not to believe in evolution in the first place.

I preach to Ben and Birdy heavily and often, because I want them to see our political beliefs as a natural extension of our scientific interests.

"We've adapted to the point where, whether we're gay or straight, we understand how to have or not have babies, which is the healthiest thing for human beings." Reproductive technology is adaptive for replicating the species; reproductive freedom is adaptive for women's health and population control. It makes perfect sense to them.

"Also karate," Birdy says. "Karate is *totally* adaptive for girls and women because it keeps you"—here she kicks her leg out and *aiiiiiis* fiercely—"safe." Indeed.

"Clearly," I explain, "justice and helping other people are adaptive." We see where caring only about money or your own self has gotten us: a world of drowning polar bears, slave labor, illness, the bogglingly unjust distribution of wealth.

Mostly, though, we don't speak in philosophical abstractions. We just like to solve evolutionary logic puzzles. Maybe it's the way other families talk about God: we are awestruck. Milkweed blows far and wide like a botanical floozy. Acorns thunk straight down beneath the sheltering oaks. "They must grow better if they're close to their moms," Birdy theorizes from my lap. A pomegranate stuns us, its seeds packed together like a ruby-filled auditorium. "Maybe it attracts the birds so that the tree can get them to poop out its seeds all over the place." Probably it does.

"Poor berries," Ben sighs. "They didn't plan on the sewer system, all us humans just flushing their seeds down." I picture—but don't mention—the related phenomenon of jizz-soaked teenage Kleenex, like so much potential life sneezed away. Ben thinks for a minute, toilets flushing over his head like lightbulbs, then asks, "What about poop?"

I laugh. "What *about* poop?"

"Why does poop smell bad, do you think?" Ben asks, then answers himself, "Probably so you won't eat it." We picture an entire race of sickened people dying off because their poop smelled like Rice Krispie Treats.

But really? Evolution is nature at its most enchanted: the beaker of science fizzing over with magic. It is logic and mystery, life and death, the omniscience of a god but without the burning-in-hell morality. Without any morality at all, actually. Ben, considering our resident swivel-headed, night-vision barn owl and the big-eared, nose-twitching mice, muses, "Nature just lets them duke it out. They both adapted for what they need to be able to do—chase or get away—and then they just do their best."

And so do we, given that we are programmed to be here and then not: to die one day, despite how ferociously attached we may be to life. At the top of a fire tower, after a lovely and vigorous hike, Ben wondered recently about death. "It's funny," he said. "I mean, it's obviously adaptive for the species as a whole for people to die. Otherwise you'd just have, like, a bazillion people everywhere, fighting over everything. But then, how did nature select for death? Because dead people? They were dead. They couldn't exactly pass along the *dying* trait."

"Whoa," says a fellow hiker, a stranger to us, raising his disturbed eyebrows at my pretty, pink-cheeked son. "Deep."

When I ask Ben what has prompted this revelation, he says, "Being kind of tempted to jump off the fire tower." Oh. "But then knowing I would die if I did. I guess it's adaptive for me personally to not want to die." I guess it is. I think about teenagers everywhere, the danger that their will to thrive will ebb treacherously away. It's basic, Ben's sense that dying is not in his own best interest, but it strikes me now as almost unutterably precious. A friend of Michael's killed himself when Ben was two, and I held his mother while she vowed to never be happy again. If one of the kids were in danger, and I could, I would lie on the floor by their bedside forever. I would hold Ben's or Birdy's hand until the day I died, if I thought that would keep them tethered here.

I expected to be the kind of parent who cared a lot about grades and colleges, success of all kinds, but I'm turning out to care more about the kids simply *being*. Happiness too, of course, although sometimes plain survival seems a big enough goal. Standing with the kids at the top of this tower, I cross my fingers and send up a kind of evolutionary prayer. We may be programmed to want our offspring to live to reproduce themselves—but it just feels like love.

How to Die of Boredom

"Mama, isn't Pucely the puceliest pucely you ever did puce?" Pucely—a derivative of *pussy*—is what Birdy calls the cat. She is in love with the cat. ("Oh my god!" she cries, rushing at houseguests with the cat in her arms, her nose buried in his fur. "You have *got* to smell my pussy!") Now she is lying on our couch on her back, bare-chested in shorty pajama bottoms. She appears to be watching the ceiling fan. "Isn't he, Mama?"

"He is."

"But isn't he the *very* puceliest?"

"The very," I say. "Do you want me to help you find something to do?"

"No." She scratches her mosquito-bitten ankles. "I don't want to do anything." At least not anything but gurgle in the back of her throat, a long, low sound that's like a cross between growling and gagging.

I used to make that exact same sound. I also used to make

a different sound, using a lollipop that I sucked vibratingly against the inside of my cheek. And one through my trumpeted-together lips, cheeks puffed out, that sounded like a grass whistle being blown by an elephant, but softly. "Mom, she's doing it again." I drove my older brother crazy—but no crazier than I drove myself, so it seemed fair enough.

"Only boring people are bored," the expression goes, and it's true. But also, bored people are boring. It's like a kind of behavioral humidity: a vague clamminess that drapes itself around you like a cloak knitted from the damp wool of torpor. Bored people complain and make weird mouth sounds and, if it's the 1970s, memorize the *Sears Wish Book* like they expect to be tested on it. *(Training bras, page 23. Barbie styling head, real pretend makeup sold separately, page 60.)* Also, there's the nausea. I don't mean that in some kind of Sartrian existential way—just that my memories of childhood boredom are often twinned with my memories of feeling like I might barf.

For example: the record player. Home with the flu, my brother and I would sprawl on the living room floor while the Beatles' *Red Album* turned around and around on the hi-fi; we lay back-down on the carpet or cheek-down on the wood; we watched the dizzying vinyl; we studied the liner notes, like British Invasion scripture that we already knew by heart. We had a comprehensive mental catalog of the lyrics, even if we didn't understand them. (Did you know, for instance, that "Norwegian Wood" is about something less like the Scandinavian forest I always pictured than like Swedish birch furniture? Me either.) It was the only record that we had, besides our parents' off-Broadway soundtracks, and listening to it was not the background to what we were doing; it was what we were doing. "Love Me Do," "Paperback Writer," "Day Tripper," "Eleanor Rigby" (was her *actual face* in a jar by the door?). To hear those songs even now is to be plunged into a kind of queasy ennui born of repetition crossed with both tedium and illness. Bang, bang, Maxwell's silver hammer came down upon my head— but dully.

And then there was the car. Road trips meant a single sickening piece of original-flavor Trident and listening to my parents listen to the metallic top-of-the-hour news jingle. (*Dee-deedle-deedle-dee.* "1010 WINS. You give us twenty-two minutes, we'll give you the world." *Dee-deedle-deedle-dee.*) If it was raining, you could lean your cheek against the glass to watch the drops gather and skid, gather and skid, the boredom itself gathering up into a kind of carsickness that occasionally had to be barfed out the window.

Boredom is like a fever dream, like the way you feel staring at the wallpaper's repeated pattern while you lie sweaty in your sickroom, listening to the clinking silverware and muted laughter of life happening elsewhere. Bored thoughts flap around like a fish on the deck of a sailboat that's going nowhere in a windless bay. "But sometimes it feels good to be bored, right?" I ask the kids now, because I am thinking about it, and Ben says, "I think if it feels good, then that's not boredom. It's the difference between wanting to not do anything, which is nice, versus there not being anything you want to do, which is being bored." Boredom is that agitated space between relaxation and action; dialed down, it can become a pleasant kind of inertia or a meditative stillness, where it feels good to sit quietly with your own thoughts; cranked up a notch, it can produce creative release. But that middle place is the boredom itself—restlessness with no movement. A dull and desperate longing for something else.

It's a strange kind of luxury, boredom—a luxury full of loss. Read the *Little House on the Prairie* books with your kids, and you just can't help envying the absence of boredom: they are simply too busy starving to death and having a fire-baked potato explode into their eye and chasing locusts off their crops to experience a moment's ennui. The kids like to mock them: "We each got an orange and a wooden button and it was the best Christmas ever!" But they envy the inherent meaningfulness of their lives, these children who were never stuck at a birthday party sticking foam die cuts to a visor with tacky glue. Even my own childhood now feels quaintly creative: we did not have endless bags of rainbow-colored chenille stems to bend and discard; we had my dad's actual white pipe cleaners, and you could take just enough to shape a pair of glasses—five—before he'd notice them missing. Then, when you were done, you had to bend them back straight so he could actually use them. We had regular beige oval rubber bands and tinfoil and *101 Uses for a Dead Cat,* which I read while laughing Fiddle Faddle out of my nose.

My kids are not so different: Ben, who can spend an entire day studying *Far Side* comics in his pajamas or picking Joni Mitchell songs out on the piano. Or Birdy, who eventually thuds to the carpet from her cat-talking, fan-watching stupor and is motivated by this act of gravity to get out the colored pencils and draw a picture of her Care Bears jigsaw puzzle. Then she builds a LEGO battleship. Then she wanders outside to arrange bark and moss into a house for the fairies, which she situates next to a toadstool "in case it rains and they need an umbrella."

I am not trying to sound like one of those crafty-mamas who suggest projects that make you want to stick a crochet hook into your eye: the kind you bookmark one day because you think that putting out a wooden bowl of felt gnomes sounds like a good idea ("Felt gnomes?" you add vaguely to your to-do list), but then you unbookmark it the next when you realize that the Wool Playthings Bowl is supposed to get refilled every morning with a different inspiring and felt-based activity and it is just too fucking much to deal with. You do have to learn boredom, learn to live with it, to manage it with the power of your own mind, without recourse to video games or bungee jumping or sniffing glue or starting a nuclear war or date-raping your roommate's girlfriend. The most dangerous people we know are the least able to sit still, to be inside an absence of motion. They are the most inclined to leave their families, to be addicts, to keep the TV on twenty-four hours a day, to kill themselves. To manage boredom quietly? That's one of life's great skills: to allow its nothingness to resolve into wonder, imagination, illumination, or mindfulness, like a blurry picture that focuses suddenly into beauty. It's a kind of inoculation against the dangerous kind of restlessness.

And also, it prepares you for having kids: what to expect when you weren't expecting your whole life to turn into *Waiting for Godot*, with Godot himself turning out to be almost as boring as the waiting. Captive under a nursing baby, you call upon all your car-sitting skills, all your floor-lying practice. The baby poops and cries and spits up into your bra, and it is all one big long meditation, halfway between tedium and franticness. ("Wake me if I actually do anything," Ben said recently, watching a very long video we'd taken of him as a newborn, kicking microscopically on his changing table.) The baby wants to play Candy Land and Hi Ho! Cherry-O and some weird zoo game where you're both dying dolphins, and you breathe in and out slowly through your nose and notice the way the sunlight is catching the down along those ripe peaches of her biceps. The baby wants to read *Maisy Goes to Bed* and *Maisy's Morning on the Farm* and *Where Is Maisy?* and your brain threatens to contract and shrivel into a dried pea rattling around your skull, but instead you inhale the baby's summer-smell scalp that is pressed fragrantly against your face (and also you occupy your mind with estimating Lucy Cousins's net worth). The falling-asleep baby wants you to scratch her mosquito bites, and when you say you'd really prefer not to, she snatches your hand in her own and uses it as a disembodied scratcher, dragging your nails across her stomach and forearms until the darkly lashed eyes flutter and close, the beloved rose of her face open and slack in sleep.

The baby, bored, wants first to clobber you with her berserkness ("Booty dance, booty dance, booty dance shakes a booty in your face!") and then to talk boringly about the cat some more. "He's pretty pucely, right, Mama?"

"Please, honey."

"I know. But, Mama?"

"Birdy?"

"What if Pucely forgot that he hadn't pooped yet? And then he pooped on your face!" "Yup," I say. "That would be something."

"Right?" she says, excited. "Right? What if he pooped *right on your face!*"

"Do you need me to help you find something to do?" I ask again, and she says, "No. I'm pretty busy."

IV

INQUIRING

How to Share a Beating Heart

I am thinking soulfully of the U2 song, but what the kids are thinking of is poop. "Gosh, I don't know," Birdy is saying. She's almost seven now. "You'd have to sit and sit and wait and wait and just be so bored while the other person was pooping." I picture us in the gas-station bathroom just yesterday, me leaning against the wall of the stall, breathing through my mouth, eager to get back on the road, while Birdy grunted and groaned and wound toilet paper around and around her hand.

"You're right," I say now. "I bet it can be pretty boring."

"But you'd never be lonely," Ben sighs—Ben, this tender-hearted ten-year-old who still bolts into our bedroom in the dead of night, driven by a loneliness that beats in his body like a second heart. "Though it *could* be kind of hard to learn to swim."

We're talking about conjoined twins. My children are, as I was and am still, a little obsessed with imagining that doubled life. It makes sense, given the way conjoined twins offer a kind of de facto case study of personhood. Would you still be you if you were your own self in a shared body? Your independent will in a dependent package? The mother of conjoined teens Abigail and Brittany Hensel says it so beautifully: "They're two girls wrapped in the same blanket." This particular pair of sisters each has a head and a heart, but they share their other limbs and organs: one liver, one uterus, two arms, two legs. Ask them if they have two heads and they roll their eyes, say, "No." Because, *duh,* they each have a single head.

And I know this because up late in a motel room, Michael and I watched the Discovery Channel special about them turning sixteen and learning to drive. These happy, fearless Minnesota kids with their shiny ponytails and spunk, bickering over when to signal and turn. My god, can you imagine your kids sharing *arms and legs?* It's hard enough for mine to share Laffy Taffy. You can't help admiring the parents with their midwestern absence of nonsense: these are kids with household chores and sturdy egos. You can't help wishing for that kind of confidence and character for your own. In fact, we almost woke ours to watch with us—they would have loved these girls—but then we didn't know how to feel. It was such a guilty pleasure, this sating of our own voyeuristic curiosity. There they are, so sassy, so teen-glossy, in their cute Aéropostale tank top; there they are, e-mailing their friends, doing each other's hair, playing softball, stopping at school lockers to gossip and giggle. When Brittany says that they plan to be moms, but then snaps at the camera that when and whom they date "is none of the world's business," you feel slapped, as if she knew that you were just then wondering about that very thing.

Which is how I always felt as a kid reading *Very Special People: The Phenomenal Bestseller That Reveals the Real Lives of Human Oddities—Their Loves and Triumphs.* This is a book that I rummaged from a bookshop bargain bin and then spent countless summer afternoons poring over while all my little ten-year-old friends were braiding lanyard key chains and swimming in each other's pools. Given my own personality, the attraction to human oddities was really no great mystery. But then here was a book that, like pornography, invited you to stare at the very things from which you knew you were supposed to look away: extra and missing limbs, beards on ladies, folks who were microscopically tiny or wildly humongous. The Mule-Faced Woman. The Dog-Faced Boy. The Elastic-Skin Man.

There were photographic plates of all of them, all uncomfortably riveting, but only the conjoined twins opened up a can of existential worms. You'd still be you with three legs or no legs, after all; you'd be you even if you were the limbless Caterpillar Man, rolling cigarettes with your lips, or if you were featured hirsutely in the chapter "Hairy, Hairy People" (as I doubtless will be soon). But what if your body were not yours alone? What about the saxophone-playing Hilton sisters, joined at the spine? What about the scribbly-named Radica and Doodica from Orissa, India, connected at the sternum? "When one took medicine, the other felt its effect" was a claim that struck—and stuck with—me. Even then it felt like a metaphor, though I wasn't sure for what. Compassion, maybe? It was a sibling trait I sorely lacked. Somewhere deep down, I worried that my own brother could have lain writhing on the floor and I would have hopped over him to yoink the last Fudgsicle from the freezer.

Like that of my own kids now, my curiosity was often scatological in nature. The same way I wondered where Laura and Mary Ingalls pooped when they were snowed in for shockingly cheerful months on end, or where the astronauts pooped when they floated around in their vacuum-packed capsule, I wondered about the Tocci brothers, who, the book pointed out, shared a rectum. Or Chang and Eng Bunker, who, married to a pair of sisters, fathered twenty-one children between them. And there's just no getting around the twenty-one certain instances of conjoined *doing it* required by that count of offspring.

For my own kids, though, it's not sex they're curious about. It's the umbrella category *privacy*—someone else snatching a peek at your nethers, say—that gets them. "For me?" Birdy says over her plate of spaghetti. "The worst thing if you were a joined twin? You couldn't be alone to go to the bathroom." Really? *That's* the worst thing? I scroll through the seven years of her life and wonder how many times out of a hundred she has yelled from the bathroom for company, wonder how many times out of a hundred I have actually finished my own wiping and flushed before she barged in.

"I know exactly what you mean," Ben is saying now. "What if you pulled down your pants, and you were, like, *Hey, everyone, come and look at my penis!* Then you'd be showing everyone *your brother's penis* too!" Ben thinks for a moment, absentmindedly drinking out of his sister's water glass. "But I guess you wouldn't really do that. You just couldn't. Being a conjoined twin would be good that way—I mean, it would make you a better person, a kinder person. You wouldn't always get what you wanted." Another moment of quiet drinking follows. "Not that you do anyways," he adds, which seems somehow to be the point exactly.

Maybe Ben is trying to think of himself as unfettered and independent, but it's a fantasy that keeps getting messed up by his identification with conjoined twins. For better or worse, Ben's life is conjoined with that of his parents and sister. "Or what if you're on a road trip," he's saying now, "and one of you has to use the bathroom, but it's not actually the best time to stop and find a bathroom?"

"Um, honey?" I say, picturing our various national tours of fast-food-restaurant toilets. "That's basically every road trip our family has ever taken."

He laughs but can't stop with his conjoined case studies. "Or, like, at fairs, if one person wanted to go on the roller coaster and the other didn't? That would be kind of hard." Yes, that would be kind of hard: I know this, since these two kids insist on each other's company on the merry-go-round or Tilt-A-Whirl but rarely agree on which rides to try. "Or on a trip? If one person wanted to go to a clam shack but the other wanted, like, *barbecue?*"

"Isn't that kind of what it's like for us?" I ask gently, and Ben laughs again.

"Oh, yeah, right! It's not like I'm just eating alone in a clam shack because that's what I wanted!" I think about the Hensel twins saying, so beautifully simply, "We take turns a lot." Exactly.

Birdy can't help taking her visions of conjoinedness to accidentally absurd end points. "What if you just had *one brain* and *one face* and *one body?*" Her eyes are wide with the shock of imagination.

"Um, Birdy?" Ben says. "Then you'd just be a regular single person."

"Oh, right!" Birdy laughs.

But I understand. She's testing out her difference from us. After years of behaving transparently, kids learn at a certain point that the movie screens of their minds play for them and them alone. Privacy and independence come on suddenly, like a sleeper wave of separation, and children experience this with simultaneous relief and dread. Birdy is different from us—connected, but apart—and after an umbilical fetus-hood and a nursling babyhood, this seems to be hard to grasp. I explain to her about the way Chang and Eng mixed first-person singular and plural in utterances like "We am Chang-Eng." It actually reminds me of Birdy herself as a comically pronoun-challenged toddler, never knowing if, as a speaker, she was "I" or "you." "Are you sleepy?" you'd ask her, and she'd reply, heartbreakingly, "You am."

Thinking about conjoined twins is somehow making concrete for us the family condition of connection and compromise, the childhood condition of separation and dependence, the parental condition of empathy and encumberedness. It's not that conjoined twins exist as a metaphor, of course; they're not simply a screen onto which we get to project our curiosity and philosophical questions. One egg split into two consciousnesses, that's why they're here, and you only have to watch the conjoined Hensel girls for one minute to grasp their fundamentally unabstract humanness. I'm thinking now of a still photo of them as little girls—a black-and-white picture of them in a swimsuit by the pool, with their frightened faces, their arms wrapped protectively around each other, while a little boy gapes at them from the water. And what I feel, looking at that photo, is what it must be like to be their parents. What it is like to be any parent. The way you ache when they ache, the way you experience their stomachaches or heartaches or fear in your very self. It's as if, having once been placentally connected to your beating heart, having once inhabited your actual body, your children continue to live there with you. For better and worse, you are never alone again. Parental love defies your apartness from another person. With a pair of small, beloved feet pressed hot against my belly, I have burned with a fever not my own. *When one took medicine, the other felt its effect.* This love is an affliction, a true human oddity. I have never been so conjoined in all my life.

"We am Birdy-Mama," my daughter teases from my lap.

But then Ben is saying suddenly, "Oh, gosh. Another thing? If one of them dies?" *Then the other will die too.* I hear it before he even says it—think of Eng dying hours after he felt Chang's fatal coldness, his heart broken literally and figuratively by the broken heart of his brother. He refused to be separated, even then, even if it meant saving his own life. I think of parents everywhere—the feeling you have that you'd die if your child died, though you wouldn't. You'd grieve and live and perhaps even thrive in your truncated self, though the ache of the missing part would never leave you. This is an individual feeling, yes, but one that exceeds the beating of a single heart. My eyes fill with tears. Only what Ben actually says is "I mean, you'd have to, like, drag around a—yuck—dead body everywhere you went." He shudders, adds, "Gross," and I am reminded for the umpteenth time that we have shared a body, this child and I. I have imagined him almost as a second self, but then, like Chang and Eng, we are two different people after all.

How to Have Complicated Feelings

"Is that your husband?" The ER nurse is pointing to Michael, who is snoring softly and muttering beside me. We've been here for hours, and for hours I've returned my lips to his scalding forehead to see if he is still feverish, which he still is. In just a little while longer, we'll find out that what he has is a severe case of strep, and he will swallow the prescribed pills, and I will finally put my lips to a cool, quietly sleeping forehead. But for now the nurse's face is creased with compassion and weariness—she is waiting—and it's not really the right time to tell her about Michael's gentle strength: the way he rocked our children in the sling for hours on end while he did his anatomy homework, the babies peacefully breathing across his broad chest.

Ben and Birdy are home asleep with their grandma, everything I love most in the world split between that house and this hospital in a way that makes me feel a little brittle with luck.

But because the kids aren't sick or even here, the whole experience is oddly—how shall I put this?—*relaxing*. Nobody wants to drink out of the viral water fountain or piece together the pox puzzles. Nobody is weeping over the possibility of a blood test or panicking at the sight of a needle. Nobody is terrified, not even me. Michael sleeps; I alternate between a mild kind of hand-to-the-hot-forehead fretting and a peaceful confidence that all will be well again. I need to pee, but I don't want to leave the room. I am too hot myself, but I don't want to make a karmic commitment to being here by unzipping my down vest. I want a cup of coffee but don't want to be the kind of person who would abandon her feverish partner to go and fetch it.

I can't remember the last time Michael was sick. The famous Martha's Vineyard clam-poisoning incident, maybe, when he was suddenly barfing bivalves into our friends' peonies while Birdy dangled from his chest in the front pack. But earlier tonight, as he bunched himself up on his hands and knees the way you do when you're, say, in labor and trying to extricate yourself from your own crazy body, I asked him to let me take him to the hospital. He was all lucid reassurance then. "Oh, no," he said from beneath the pillow he was pressing over his head. "I'm okay. Really." But a little later he'd said, "Actually, maybe that's not a bad idea, the hospital." "Are you kidding?" I said. "Oh my god! Are you *that* sick?" And he said, "Oh, no, no. I'm fine." And then, "But let's just go anyways."

Ben was awake still, and naturally fretful. The same Ben who has cheerfully shared his dreams about Michael's demise. "I dreamed you died," he said once, snuggled happily in the bed between Michael and me, "and, weirdly, I wasn't that sad." Michael, being Michael, laughed and was offended not at all— making him different from me. Once Birdy said, "I dreamed that I slid down a big giant scary slide and Daddy caught me at the bottom, and, Mama, you weren't even *anywhere.*" "Oh, yeah?" I said. "Well, *Daddy* didn't even stay awake to hear the end of your dream." And Birdy listened to Michael's gentle snoring and laughed. "I would have been there too, at the bottom, in real life," I said, and Birdy shrugged and said abstractedly, "Maybe."

A friend of ours once said, when I was pregnant with Birdy and worried about shifting family dynamics, "Love doesn't divide. It multiplies." I love that saying. But also? Sometimes love kind of divides. Ben grimaces if you ask whether he pictures a partner and kids in his future. "Oh, god, no," he says. "I'm just going to live in an RV in your driveway and run my little sandwich restaurant." "It's okay," I said to my mom, when she'd started to argue that his plan seemed unsound. "He's got a while to figure it out."

When Michael is away overnight, Ben climbs into our bed in a way that I can only describe as proprietary. "Since Daddy's gone," he says, shrugging, and snuggles in. "I mean, I miss him. But, hey! Silver linings, right?"

Silver linings exactly. In the ER now, it's not the right time to explain what a funny contradiction Michael is, a hockey-playing massage therapist, or how just last week he laid his hands on a friend's father while he lay dying in hospice, how the old man fell into a deep and quiet sleep. Home again later this afternoon, his fever starting to break, Michael will come frailly downstairs, where the children will be a little shy, as if this pale and rumpled person is someone they don't wholly know. My mother and I will take Birdy to watch Ben's chorus sing "Jerusalem" with a hundred other people in a beautiful chapel, and the swell of the organ, of voices young and old, will leave us in tears. In forty-eight hours, my caretaking impulse will snap abruptly off, like a thrown switch, a whistle blown, my time card punched at the end of my shift, and I will become impatient with both Michael and the pace of his recovery. "Need anything?" I'll say briskly from the doorway, and Michael will look at my face and say, wisely, "No. I'm good." I will feel, in fact, not very well myself, like someone is shaking my hand with a joy buzzer, only it's not my hand, it's my sinus cavity, and I will feel achy and tired, like I need to be put to bed with a hot-water bottle on my neck and a cold beer in my hand, despite the fact that my temperature has soared only up to 99.

The nurse doesn't know that I'm strangely euphoric now, sitting here thinking about how lucky I am to have so much to lose—my rock, my mystery, the love of my life—that I'm sitting here thinking *in sickness and in health. I will,* I think. *I do.* But all I can say is *yes.* "Yes," I say. "That's my husband."

How to Be a Bad Capitalist

"So socialism means that everyone shares everything?" Birdy is trying to understand why I refer to our cooperative summer arrangement as Socialist Friend Camp, the period of the summer when five or six families take turns having all the kids for a day so that everyone else can work—a tradition that makes me feel, smugly, like we are totally screwing the Man. "And why do you always say it that way?" She means *Slavically*.

I sigh. "It's hard to explain," I say, and this is true. The accent is only part of it. Really what I want to do is move through my suburban life in full Karl Marx costume, complete with bushy gray beard, bushy gray hair, and *The Communist Manifesto*. If I were to be historically accurate, I would also have a wife somewhere, frying up platters of bratwurst for me and my comrades.

There has never been a more disastrously extreme divide between the rich and the poor. Even though there's enough to go around, it doesn't go around. It's easy for me to point my revolutionary finger: *There. Bazillionaire! Bad.* But what about right here, in my warm, comfortable house with rooms galore and cupboards lined with food? "In a second I would give it all up, I would, if that's the direction the world were headed," I say, and I mean it. But when the children say, "So let's," I hesitate. I barely have time to nag Michael to mow our lawn; the fomenting of a movement and then the actual moving feel beyond the scope of my bourgeois energy level.

But sometimes it can be a little devastating, the sweetness we cultivate in our children, our insistence that they share their Zhu Zhu Pets and Sour Patch Kids. Why even bother teaching them the values of sharing and cooperation when our national ethos is the hoarding of food and medicine, land and resources, like the good capitalists that we are? Maybe we're just helping them get all that pesky sharing out of the way so it doesn't burden them later, when they're clambering over one another toward the teetering heights of personal wealth.

Isn't it weird to imagine kids treating each other the way grown-ups do? Pimping out the labor of their peers, CEOing the babysitting and lawn mowing to exploit one another for profit? Some kids unfettered in their wealth and greed, piggy banks overflowing, while other kids, the ones doing the actual work, can't make a living wage? Ha ha ha! Oh, right, it's not actually funny.

I teach the kids various Marxist principles: people should feel connected to the work they do; they should work as much as they can and get as much as they need. But it doesn't help that

I am, as always, fuzzy on the details of my political passion. Everything I know about alternatives to capitalism I know from the Woody Allen movie *Bananas*. Also from growing up in the age of Cold War propaganda. Remember how Nadia Comaneci's gold-medal floor routines were interspersed with footage of her parents waiting grayly in assorted sleeting bread lines? My own Russian grandmother seemed to spend the 1970s making borscht and sending relatives home to the mother country with suitcases full of jeans. "You vill sell, yes?" The poor Communists didn't even have *jeans!* Those glum kerchief-headed kids, waiting denimlessly for their heavy Soviet loaves.

I want my kids to maintain their optimistic vision of utopian justice without misleading them about the fact that there aren't such great examples of it in human history—what with the waiting in line for tickets to the toilet-paper line, as one comedian put it. Or at least no examples that I can explain very well. Sweden, for example. What actually goes on in Sweden, besides making meatballs and becoming supermodels? Do they stand in IKEA lines for their national allotment of Smorssgläben side tables? I have no idea. Beyond the better maternity leave, health care, and some kind of national right to blondness, I don't know much. Which doesn't seem to dam the stream of opinions pouring from my political face hole.

We get out Monopoly like good citizens, so that we can learn about private property and screwing everybody. "You'd be able to get rich," I explain to my losing children, "if you weren't already so poor!" *Suckers.* On principle, we also play

Harvest Time, which is gentle and cooperative: we help one another hurry our crops into the root cellar before winter comes, but it is so frankly dull that we end up with our foreheads on the table, groaning, even while our naturally collaborative Birdy is offering us corn and carrots because she's got more than she needs. "Make a curry," she suggests.

The kids talk about what they would wish for if they could have anything, distinguishing between *just-for-being-selfish* wishes (our own personal soda machine with soda in it that you would actually let us drink) and *the real wish you would wish if you only had one wish* (justice). "If you had limitless money," Ben always prompts me, "then you could get the stuff you want and still buy everyone everything they need, right?" He pictures himself with stacks and stacks of million-dollar bills, glad-handing his way to health and happiness for all, even as the Coke dispenser is being installed in our new billiards room. I explain that a radical redistribution of wealth is more complicated—more like beads moved around on an abacus than extra rows of beads added onto it—but it's not what I actually picture. *Justice:* a cool hand smoothing the forehead of our feverish world.

People are always quick to remind me that communism has never worked. And, sure, Cuba, China, the Soviet Union: too little fun, too much corruption—plus the executing of everybody who wasn't already incarcerated. But what about capitalism? It does seem to sleet less now in Eastern Europe, what with everyone's access to bright pastels, the denim trousers without borders. But it's hard to argue that capitalism is *working*, exactly. Life, liberty, and the pursuit of crap you don't need and also the Pottery Barn lidded baskets to store it all in. I'm glad I'm not, say, a *serf*—but at least with feudalism, nobody was tricked into thinking that anyone could be king if they only worked hard enough or got a basketball scholarship.

Across the table from me now, Ben is eating a piece of blueberry crumb cake and showing me his fifth-grade homework. "It's a compare-and-contrast chain about Wakaima and the Clay Man," he explains, "which is a story about a lazy rabbit who makes an elephant do all the work on the farm. We're supposed to show how it's like a real-life situation." He has, I see, described the story as a fable about factory owners and exploited workers. I have never been prouder. *Workers of the world, unite!*

"Why are you writing about my homework?" Ben asks pleasantly, crumbs spraying as he leans over to look at my computer screen. "I'm writing about talking to kids about capitalism," I tell him, and he says, "Wait, what's capitalism again?"

Did I mention that Ben's life goal is to own the world's biggest casino? And also, you know, to promote justice. "When really rich people come and lose money," he explains, "I'll give that money away to an organization."

I'm not really surprised. It must be confusing to be the child of such a split-personality family. We pick through bunches of organic kale when the world is full of people who aren't eating at all—when across town from us there are mothers picking through outdated cans in the food pantry, and across the world from us there are mothers rocking dying babies. What if my own children were ill in my arms, stilled by malnutrition or malaria, and I looked across the globe and saw people like us, in our cozy New England Cape, with our shoes for every season and our compost heaped with uneaten food? I don't know what to think. It's not right, living this way. It's not fair. So we teach our kids to share because we know it's the only way to thrive, all of us.

How to Make Do with Abundance

Lucky for us, out here on the prairie, we're immune to the bad economy! So accustomed are we to the bleak eating of turnips and plucking of locusts from our withering crops that really, what's a little widespread financial downturn? Oh, wait. That's Laura Ingalls Wilder's life. But I'm thinking of her because Michael has just passed through the kitchen and laughed at me: "Nice work, Ma." I'm standing over a steaming pot, an apron tied around me, my hands dyed purple from the wild grapes I'm stirring into jam. Seriously.

It's true that, given the nearby fact of Trader Joe's, our life does not depend on the successful canning of summer's bounty. But I love the old-fashionedness of it. Also the frugality. And something else that's harder to explain. Purpose, maybe. It's one thing to drag your kids out for a walk, when the goal is a view or a handful of acorns. You seduce them all the way up a mountain and back with lollipop rings and Goldfish, with praise and a kind of performative joy—"This is so fun! Right? Right? Isn't it great?"—even though part of you would really rather be back at home with your coffee and the Sunday crossword. But you want to be outside, or you *want to* want to, and you want the kids to be outside, and so everyone is outside, moving around with the goal of moving around outside.

That's fine, but foraging is better. Foraging gives shape and meaning to what is otherwise a weirdly pointless desire to walk nowhere and walk back. Foraging is like a plain old walk crossed with an Easter egg hunt crossed with a fine-dining experience. Crossed, of course, with the possibility of being fatally poisoned. But it's worth it. We're hardwired to find food. A neuroscientist I talked to is convinced that our brains reward us with nice little hits of feel-good dopamine when we look for, and find, things we can eat in the wild. So basically we're getting free autumn olives and oyster mushrooms and Concord grapes. And also we're getting high. So we've got that going for us, which, to quote Bill Murray in *Caddyshack,* is nice.

Plus, what could be slap-you-in-the-face fresher than a pile of produce you harvested from the forests and waysides? Especially when what's in the ill-named crisper at home is just a slippery bag of the Oldest Living Confederate Broccoli.

Birdy loves the illicit thrill of bending down and putting things into her mouth. After living so much of her seven years with the specific injunction to not do exactly this, the irony is not lost on her. She touches a gentle finger to a jewelweed pod, which springs open into perfect green coils and releases its tasty seeds into her hand. She pops them into her mouth, chews thoughtfully, and says, "Yum. They taste like walnuts. Which I don't actually like. But these are good."

"We could totally be on a reality show!" she decides, a little while later. "Survival in nature! As long as it was September, or maybe June. And as long as it only lasted for one afternoon. We could always bring snacks anyway, just in case."

Come spring, we'll tromp through the woods, cramming leaves into our mouths like scurvied cave people blinking in the fresh light. Everything will taste like the color green, and nothing will have a flavor you'd describe as mild. Dandelion greens are as punishingly bitter as a pill; garlic mustard tastes first pleasantly of cabbage and then shockingly of the acetone in nail polish remover; arrow-shaped sorrel makes us pucker and wink; burdock is hairy and astringent. Chewing these wild things, you cannot forget for one second that what you are is *alive.* Munching foraged food has so little in common with spacing out over a bowl of Cheerios that it seems funny that both activities are called *eating.*

But for now, it is autumn nuts and seeds and berries, the grapes pulled down in big buggy clusters, the skins so taut and tart they burst open and make your lips itch. Stirring them at the stove makes me too pleased with myself. I know that. *I'm this kind of mother,* I think happily, and then immediately flush with shame over my own vanity and falseness, given that I am also the kind of mother who lathers up her hair with one hand so that she doesn't have to put her beer down in the shower.

I think about the Ingallses—how they were barely surviving all the time, how grateful the kids were to get a single orange for Christmas, how little they had, how happy they were. Night fell, and Pa played his fiddle, and the children popped corn and crunched apples, everybody rosy and smiling in the firelight. *I don't know if that pleasure was so different from mine,* I think, and then I know that it's not true. This pleasure, mine, is prairie frugality crossed with suburban abundance. I am not worried about my kids being actually hungry. The land around us is not locust-plagued, but—to speak more of global now than prairie then—it is also neither war-torn nor drought-ridden. We will not need to flee this place, or open our last jar of food in February, terrified. So when Birdy darts in to taste the still-warm jam from my wooden spoon, it is pure pleasure, hers and mine. "This is the best batch yet!" she says, without even a trace of irony. Then she kisses me with her grapy lips and I experience something beautiful—something that could really only be called *grace.*

V

LAUNCHING

How to Hang by a Thread

One minute, we're skipping through the sunshine, and the next we're lodged in the belly of the diagnostic beast. It's the X-rays that happen first—only we're not actually thinking *first* because we don't understand yet what's ahead of us. We're in the radiology department that's just down the hall from our pediatrician's office, which is the comforting medical equivalent of the girl next door. How bad can it be if they don't even make you leave the neighborhood?

Still, I sit in the waiting room beneath the warm weight of Birdy, breathing in the summer smell of seven-year-old braids, and I wonder if our lives are about to change. Is there going to be a *before* this moment and an *after?* The radiology order is sweaty in my fingers. "? *Mass in chest wall*" it says, in busy-doctor scrawl. What is *mass?* That mystifying physics property that's like weight, only different: the mass of the mass is equal to something squared divided by the extent to which we can spare Birdy, which is not at all. The alliterative "malignant mass" I've heard a million times, but "benign mass" is suddenly not ringing any bells. Also, *chest wall.* Your heart is kind of counting on your chest wall to protect it, I'm guessing. It's not really supposed to have a mass in it. I'd be happier with "? *Mass in kneecap*" or "? *Mass in big toe.*" "The further away it is from your brain, the better," Ben once consoled his grandmother when she was having a squamous-cell something removed from her shin. Indeed. But it's also better the further away it is from your heart. My heart.

So far approximately four minutes have elapsed, and I'm already deranged. It will be another two and a half months before the doctors figure out what's going on.

"Abigail Newman?" The radiology technician is holding the door open, and hearing Birdy's given name, which nobody uses, makes me feel like she's in trouble. *Abigail Newman, you get in here this second! Did you leave this mass in your chest wall?* I help Birdy off with her clothes while the technician clucks over the order. "You just don't like to see stuff that's unilateral like this," she muses grimly, shaking her head. No? I concentrate on not bursting into tears by teasing Birdy about her outfit: a floor-length floral-sprigged johnny with a little lead apron tied around her waist. "All you need is a bonnet and you'd look just like Ma Ingalls!" I say, and Birdy laughs, twirls, and curtsies before sitting dead still for ten minutes so the buzzing machine can spy on her bones. "Wow," I say, looking over the tech's shoulder as a series of images appears on her computer screen. "Look at all your strong ribs! I really see why they call it a rib cage! It really does look like a cage! Doesn't it look like a cage? How fascinating!"

The optimistic patter of the worried parent! It is very exclamatory! And it continues farther down the hall, where we've now been sent for an ultrasound after the X-ray has illuminated exactly nothing. "I thought it was going to be bone," the tech has said. "But it's not—which means it's got to be soft tissue." She tried to grimace at me sympathetically, but I looked away to better thwart her pessimistic contamination. *Soft tissue.* Oh, Birdy of the softest tissue! *Soft tissue* is the Kleenex nest she made for her tiniest bear in an old walnut-shaped nut bowl. *Soft tissue* is the meatiness of her luscious thighs. "Wow!" I say instead. "We get to see all your insides working! That's a lucky thing!" You see their innards before they're born—that strange prenatal introduction to your baby via her black-and-white internal organs—and then, ideally, never again. "So, so lucky!" I repeat. And we are lucky. The ultrasound tech shows us her beating heart, the galloping wild horse of her life. But my Pollyanna muscle is strained and spent by the labor of good cheer. I know the tech can't and won't answer my questions, but still I can't help myself. "What do you think?" I ask, trying to trick her with my chummy casualness. "See anything?" "We'll let the radiologist take a look," she answers, all pleasant poker face.

We are sent back up the hall to wait, and our pediatrician finally calls us in, shrugging over the radiology reports. "They didn't see anything," she says, and I imagine for a moment that our collective hallucination has been swatted away by the empirical hand of science, like the finale of a *Scooby-Doo* mystery: *Turns out there was a hologram of a mass on the chest wall here, which had us all fooled!* "Which is good," she continues, "but weird because it's not like there's not something here." Right. The doctor and I take turns feeling Birdy up, and she giggles. "How long has she had the lump?" the pediatrician wants to know, and suddenly I'm not sure. Has it been in my peripheral awareness for a while? Maybe. But then I'd been smearing Birdy with sunscreen and there it was for sure, the lumpy, insistent fact of it, like something pushed under her skin: a doughnut hole, a bottle cap, a clot of abnormally dividing cells. The creamy ho-hum precaution of SPF 45 seemed, suddenly, malevolently, like a red herring. "I don't know," I say.

Now the doctor says the first thing that scares Birdy: "I think I'm going to send you guys to the surgeon." Birdy's wide eyes fill with tears, and the doctor is quick to reassure her. "Just because they know more about this stuff," she says. "Not because they're going to operate on you." One cherry-dip cone later, good cheer has returned to Birdyland. "Dumb lump," she says, and pats her chest affectionately with a sticky pink hand.

Our appointment is scheduled for three weeks from now. In the endless interim, we see my brother and his wife, brilliant physicians both, who examine Birdy at my request. They are heartbreakingly gentle with her, and she shows off a little under the bright light of their attention. "I call him Lumpy," she says, all casual-like, puffing out her little bare chest. "Because he's so lumpy!" They are both dismissive—they agree that it's likely some kind of a benignly anomalous growth spurt—and afterward my relief coincides with a cooling and lightening of the summer's hot, heavy skies. We also see my parents. "Whatever you do, don't mention it to them," I badger Michael in the car. "We'll tell them about it later, after it all turns out to be fine." Yet we are in their apartment maybe fifteen seconds before I blurt out, "Birdy has a lump in her chest. They don't know what it is. I'm sure it's fine. We're seeing a specialist. I don't want you to worry." I can't help it. Their concern is the psychic equivalent of someone holding my hand during the scary parts of *The Wizard of Oz.* I feel like an asshole to worry them, but I'm glad for their company.

The surgeon, when we finally see him, has a kind of blustery masculine confidence that doubtless makes him a terrible person to date, but he is an excellent one to talk to about a mass in your daughter's chest wall. We leave his office with an order for an MRI and a holistic sense of Birdy's fineness. He is not overly concerned, he has told us, and I believe him. Only here's what happens: waiting, which we must do more of now, is like a kind of diagnostic solitary confinement, corrosive to both spirit and sanity. The relief starts out vast and gleaming like a serene expanse of turquoise sea. But then all the what-ifs—the troubling turns of phrase and outside chances—rise to the surface, until the likelihood of Birdy's okayness is fully circled by sharks. The picture of health jigsaws apart into pieces again, fragments that, held up one at a time, are impossible to interpret. "'It's probably cartilage,'" I quote the surgeon back to Michael, in the middle of the night. "'But we just want to make sure there's nothing *inside* the cartilage that's making it grow like that.'"

Michael, who's floating calmly at the surface of what's most likely, which is that Birdy's fine, says, "They just need to make sure."

Right. "I'll be shocked," the surgeon has said, "if there turns out to be a malignancy." This seemed good enough at the time—great, even!—but now I hate that he said the word *malignancy* aloud, even for the purpose of dismissing it. The more time passes, the more I want to ask him approximately how often he's shocked. For all we know, a dozen things a day shock him: "I'm shocked that nobody filled the ice trays!" "I'm shocked that we're out of Special K!" "There turned out to be a malignancy? Well, color me shocked!"

There is also the fact that our MRI is not even scheduled yet. "You'll get a letter in the mail with the date and time of your scan," the surgeon's receptionist had explained. When I called after a week, it turned out that the appointment scheduler was on vacation; after two weeks, the letter mailer was. I am so profoundly falling to pieces that I'm surprised not to see that my limbs have dropped off and are strewn around the house. "Maybe I'll just go ahead and go to medical school and specialize in radiology," I say to Michael in the middle of the night. "To save time." I finally wrangle the appointment out of them. We have two more weeks to wait.

"I'm not going to Google it," I say resolutely to Michael in the middle of the night. "Don't you Google it either." Then I get up and Google it. And here is my conclusion: people don't tend to log on to the Internet to tell nice, boring stories about everything turning out just fine. Meanwhile, I can't keep my hands off of Birdy's chest. I'm like a bad date, wrapping my arms around her and groping her on the sly. I daydream about her illness and death and experience an anticipation of grief that's almost ecstatic in its clarity. I tell you this confessionally. In this twilight zone of waiting, I cannot stop imagining my own bereftness.

Brave Birdy Bluebird is what they call my daughter at her karate class, and I think about this during the MRI. Have you had one? I haven't and so I have poorly prepared Birdy for it: the noisy white and whirring tunnel that sucks her in and keeps her while she holds her breath for twenty-five courageous seconds at a time, fifteen times in forty-five minutes. Have you held your breath for twenty-five seconds? I haven't and I am doing it now because I cannot stop trying to have this experience for Birdy and it is hard. *This is your maternal empathy on crack.* I am dizzy and smiling nonstop, like a crazy person. Birdy's chin quivers at one point, and she says, near tears, "I think I might have breathed during that last one." We are alone in the room, Birdy in the tunnel in a paper dress, me squatting to hold her hand, and the Muzak version of the *Annie* soundtrack stops long enough for a disembodied voice to buzz in: "That's okay. We'll try that one again." On strict magnetic orders, I have removed my belt and earrings, but I keep picturing the metal fillings flying out of my molars into the tunnel, lodging in Birdy's skull. "At least nothing actually *hurts!*" I offer, lamely, moments before the tech comes back in with a dye-pumping, huge-needled IV. "Whatever you do, don't move while I inject you, or we'll have to do *all the pictures over again.* Okay, sweetheart?"

Across the way, they are wheeling in a tiny baby, pushing her into a different tunnel. It is not just us, I know.

On our way out, they give Birdy a coupon for a free ice cream cone from the Friendly's downstairs. "This is so lucky!" she says, thrilled, while they swirl her soft-serve, and I am so in love with her that I have to squeeze her and kiss the top of her head even though it's not enough. What I really want to do is shrink her down and stuff her into my mouth. I want to marry her. I want to buy her a present—I can see the gift shop across the hall—but then I wonder suddenly if we're going to be coming here a lot and if we'd better keep a trick or two up our sleeves just in case. I imagine wheeling Birdy down from the pediatric unit upstairs, watching her fondle the Beanies and choose one; I imagine her cheerful disbelief, "This is so lucky!"

In the Friendly's line behind us, a woman bursts into tears, and a man puts his arms around her. It is not just us.

The MRI shows—wait for it—nothing. More precisely, either more or less than nothing. The radiologist, who has never once laid eyes on the flesh-and-blood fact of my daughter, actually thinks there may be more swelling on *the other* side of her chest—a suggestion that maddeningly defies empirical evidence. We are stuck in a world of robots making their robot pronouncements. Our surgeon, who is away on vacation, communicates to his reception staff that he wants us to do an ultrasound. *Another ultrasound?* Yes. We'll get a letter in the mail with the date and time of our scan. It's like one of those awful Escher drawings, and this one is called "The Möbius Strip of Medical Imaging." We are driving around and around the diagnostic parking garage, looking for the exit sign, and we can never seem to leave the level we parked on.

Two weeks later, Birdy sits in my lap while we wait for the ultrasound. She is cracking herself up, remembering her misunderstanding at a Halloween party. "Remember how that kid was dressed up as a corpse?" she said. "I thought he was going to look like trail mix. But when I saw him in those gross sheets, I realized I was thinking of *gorp!*" She laughs, a sound like a bell but crossed with a kazoo. I am afraid, yes, but I finally—what?—wake up. I think something like *There is this, now. There's really only ever this.* I can continue to terrify myself, imagining a future with no Birdy, or I can pine for the carefree, lump-free Birdy of the past—or I can just be present for the real girl who is right in front of me and pay attention as her cheerfully unraveling braids bob against me and her little body shakes with mirth, her gap-toothed smile making her look like a radiant old man. Life isn't about avoiding trouble, is it? It's about being present, even through the hard stuff, so you don't miss the very thing you're trying so hard not to lose. I understand all at once the title of a Zen book I haven't even read: *Full Catastrophe Living.* That's what I'm doing. It's the full catastrophe, and I'm in it, and if I wait for it to be over, well, it will be over.

Another two weeks later, we watch Birdy from my parents' kitchen window, bent over a patch of chives in my mother's herb garden while my father's riding mower, running and riderless, careens down a hill toward her. We have just met with our surgeon, who reviewed the radiology reports for us and concluded that it was, as he'd suspected, a benign overgrowth of cartilage. "I am very glad there's no tumor," he said to us, and then, to the medical resident who was shadowing him, "I was very worried there was a tumor." What happened to *I would be shocked?* I felt faint from the combination of relief and retroactive fear. I hadn't even worried *enough,* it turned out! I had not fully understood the danger. "Cartilaginous exostosis" is the official diagnosis: i.e., a lump. It might get bigger when she gets bigger; it might require a brace or surgical intervention; blah blah, who cares. It is not life-threatening and so I am filled with fondness for it. Lumpy! Only now I am running outside, screaming, but the mower has already veered away and stalled in a patch of vinca under the maple tree. Birdy is standing in the sunlight, whole and unharmed. My father had stepped away for just a minute, it turns out. This is not the other shoe dropping. It is not tragic irony or doom or punishment for our interpretive failures. It is life, with loss woven into its very fabric. That's just what there is.

How to Make the Best of It

I am not a person who presumes that an unexpectedly epic layover in the Philadelphia airport is going to be some sort of a Zen-tastic lesson in being here now. In fact, I've historically been the kind of joyless, neurotic traveler who treats minor delays like major impediments to well-being: lost luggage is a sign of the coming apocalypse; snack prices are an affront to my dignity and intelligence. "Seriously? Five ninety-five for a bagel *with cream cheese?* Are they kidding? It better come with a side of gold doubloons. Thank goodness we brought those raisins from home." Poor Michael. It was probably like being stuck traveling with somebody's prim and cranky great-aunt. "Great. There's our suitcase, on the runway, *in the rain.*" Travel was all about arriving somewhere else—the getting-there like a parenthetical blur of irritatedness and free Diet Coke. And the introduction of babies to the mix did not exactly improve this situation—although it's true that we laughed a lot more, even as we whacked other passengers on the head with the car seat ("Sorry! Sorry!"), chased soggy, marauding toddlers up and down the aisle, and rummaged through our bags to deconstruct a four-hour plane trip into a thousand ten-second-long activities: mirror, keys, phone, tissues, Tampax, credit cards, lip balm. ("No, we don't eat ChapStick. Yes, you do really want to.")

But somehow the maniac babies have become these actual people who turn traveling into a party, and you're lucky you got invited. In Philly now, Ben and Birdy take each other's picture in the massage chair at Sharper Image, vibrating and screaming with laughter; they smell all the lotions and potions at the Body Shop ("Mango body butter! Passion-fruit hand sanitizer!"); they tip souvenir pens to slide the Liberty Bell from one end to the other; they sweet-talk us into splurging on smoothies and then splurging again on good fries in a bar where we sit for two hours and play the comically named dice game Farkle. ("Excuse me," the kids always say when they're losing. "I Farkled.") The whole airport is like a museum of sensory pleasures (except for the automatically flushing toilets, which still scare them), and we are sheltered, safe, and together. Getting somewhere else seems kind of beside the point.

Of course the plane itself will be a lot of fun too: the kids lure you into *SkyMall* to ogle patio drains and dog stairs, even while the newspaper sits unread in your lap, and they await their boxed snacks with anticipation bordering on awe ("I got a whole entire *package of crackers!*" "I got a whole entire *triangle of cheese!"*). I'm not saying the layover is the best part of our trip. But, then, I'm not saying it's not. *It's the journey, not the destination.* Whatever it is we're all traveling toward—love, joy, happiness—I think I'm already there.

How to Survive a Flood

"What about these?" Ben asks, and holds up a pair of empty tissue boxes. He is twelve years old, standing in our basement, ankle deep in freezing water. In ten minutes it will be midnight. "There are tons more, and if we cut them open and taped them together, maybe we could make a kind of channel." I don't have any better ideas. It has been a crazy winter. It snowed, snowed more, and then kept snowing, like snow was the new *air*. Snow piled up in drifts so high that the children tunneled a maze of snow caves through the yard and scampered through it like gerbils. Cardinals have been posing picturesquely, red against the white, like they're waiting for us to paint them. Lovely. Truly. Only now we need to build an ark. After a sudden thaw, melted snow is Niagara Falls–ing over the baseboards and, for some reason, pooling on the side of the basement where the sump pump is not. We are trying to move it across the floor, drainward.

"Oh, god, honey," I say. I am tired and despairing. "That's a great idea—but shouldn't you go to bed? I'm worried about keeping you up so late." But he's already duct-taping boxes together, and his engineer eyes are shining. "Are you kidding me?" he says. "I *love* this!" And he does. He tries the box channel, which works only briefly before sogging into uselessness. He tries taping together toilet-paper tubes, plastic clamshells, wooden blocks; he sketches solutions on a piece of cardboard; he scratches his head and taps his chin like a caricature of a person problem solving. The water rises and my husband, who is tinkering with the sump pump, sings the *Titanic* theme song in full vibrato. I look over, and he is standing in water—the same water we're standing in—plugging an extension cord into an outlet. "Honey," I say. "Don't electrocute us," and he says, "Wait, what? *Do* or *don't?*"

Obviously, I'm not precisely *happy*—but this is far from the least fun I've ever had in my life. In fact, it is strangely delightful: I can't help noticing how creative and helpful my son is, or how capable and good-natured his father is. I can't help noticing that, on the two floors above us, the house offers us all the warmth we need (with only a small caveat about the living room's leaking ceiling). I can't help noticing, in sum, how lucky we are. Given the fact that our lives are far from perfect, we do get to spend a lot of time in the glow of the silver lining. We make a lot of lemonade. Our glass is half full—even if it's not always with the exact drink we originally wanted.

Which is not to say I didn't blurt the f-word when Birdy took her helmet off after a bike ride last summer and I saw something scurry along her hairline. *What the?* It just meant that we turned Licegate into a kind of ad hoc spa retreat. I put everyone in old T-shirts before massaging warm and fragrant olive oil into their scalps. We wore shower caps for twenty-four hours, which meant, apparently, that we had to stay home, rent *Naked Gun,* and order a pizza ("Long story," I said to the delivery guy, who raised his eyebrows at our plastic-wrapped heads). One at a time I laid each person down and combed dead bugs from their hair. And I reminisced. You simply cannot gaze at your child's scalp without remembering the endless days of babes in arms: nursing babies, napping babies, rocking babies. Studying those downy whorls of hair, inhaling that otherworldly infant-head smell, and even picking idly at cradle cap—the scalps of my children are pure nostalgic topography. Infestation is not the key to happiness, but it wasn't without its pleasures.

The kids themselves are learning it too: how to harness difficulty in the service of gratitude; how to work disappointment in their minds like putty, to shape it into something new; how to spot through the darkness that glint of silver. At my parents' house, where we spent a recent weekend, Ben was briefly sick in the night, then spent the next day under the exquisite care of my mother: she propped him up in her bed and brought him Coke and Saltines on a tray while he chuckled through an ultramarathon of *SpongeBob SquarePants.* "That was one of my favorite days ever," he sighed later, and I laughed. Are the kids going to end up Pollyanna-ing their way to psychotherapy? Maybe. I can certainly picture Ben holding his own severed arm while thanking his lucky stars he started out with two. And it's all a little suspect, given that I'm half English and England seems to be the birthplace of the repressed pod people. "There's blue enough to make a Dutchman's breeches!" my mum likes to say, squinting at a tiny patch in a storm-gray sky. And I just found a card from my dear late grandmother, sent after an early miscarriage. "Chin up, darling," she wrote. "These things happen for a reason! It will doubtless all turn out for the best!" *(Be calm and carry on! Mind the gap!)* But I don't know. Rolling with the punches, making the best of it—these are such good life skills. Even now I think, gratefully, *If I'd had that baby, I wouldn't have had Ben.*

In a pond last summer, as my son rowed me around in an inflatable boat, my glasses plunked off the top of my head and into the water, then blurped down to the bottom, whence they were irretrievable. The children talk about it still. "I'm sorry you lost your glasses," Ben says. "But it was so funny to see you leap off the boat in your clothes and swim around in all that mud and grass. It might have been my favorite thing from the whole summer." It's the writer's trick: *At least you got a good story out of it.* Where would all those country singers be without their broken-down trucks and heartbreak? What would comedians joke about if they never got stuck inside a moose costume or locked out of the house naked?

I wasn't always like this, though. I used to be the person bemoaning rain on vacation instead of thanking heaven for the time off, the person feeling like we might be in a drafty spot at the restaurant instead of enjoying my nachos, the person ruing the heft of my thighs instead of exulting in the fact that they get me where I want to go (note to self: stop ruing the thighs). And I struggle still with envy, the literal and/or metaphorical craning of my head around to see who has more or better. *It should have been me who*...wrote that article about dogsledding, won a MacArthur grant, built a screen porch, ordered the calamari. Even though I want for nothing—not really. And even though I understand that if you can't enjoy what you *do* have, then you would never be happy anyway with whatever it is you think you want. The trick isn't to love your life when it's perfect. The trick is to cherish the messy beauty. Even if sometimes it's really kind of excessively messy.

Having kids is what changed me. Not just the kids abstractly, but the very fact of my first birth: a harrowing twenty-four-hour labor that ended in a placental abruption, the disappearance of the baby's heartbeat, and an emergency C-section. Later, various visitors held the warm, blanket-wrapped burrito of Ben and tried to process with me my disappointment about the birth not being of the dreamy gardenia-scented birth-canal variety, but I was too busy basking in the afterglow of miracle to feel any. "Just look at him!" I said to everyone. "I'm so lucky." You shove it out your vagina or they yank it from your abdomen—whatever. With absolute newborn perfection in my arms, with the fear of losing him still so fresh, the particulars of his escape hatch had come to matter not at all.

I know we would not be sighing gladly through a real catastrophe like hunger, grief, or discrimination. But maybe that's the point: knowing the difference. The difference between the blown-away farms north of us, where the storm raged strongest, and our own, gentle experience of a hurricane that leaves us playing candlelit board games while wind slams doors spookily around the house. "This is more fun than electricity!" Birdy said at some point, and it was true.

There is always, at the very least, the miracle of pulling air into your lungs. But there's usually more. The velvet face of a pansy, the dark crescent of your sleeping child's eyelashes, starshine. There is so much to be glad for. "If he were nice *all the time*," Birdy says, about our cranky pussycat, "we wouldn't appreciate him as much." True enough. "If we were rich," I say sometimes, when we are feeling especially broke, "we might not do some of the very things that are my *favorite* things!" Tent camping, picking wild grapes for jam, fixing broken things instead of buying new ones. "Oh, I'm sure we'd find new favorites," my husband says, and I laugh.

But for now, Ben and I have managed to wick the water across the floor with a long rope of knotted rags. It is after one in the morning. Within the week, the basement will be dry again—or, at least, as dry as it ever is—but we don't know that now. We just know that we're cold and we're tired and we're flush with our small, wet success. I kiss him in bed, and Ben is sleepy and smiling. "That was fun, right?" he says. "That was the best." And he's right. It was.

VI

FALTERING

How to Be Attached

"You poor thing," I say to him, after the morning blur of sneakers and lunch boxes has shut the door behind itself. "Are you already missing Birdy?" He smiles, his face pinkly gentle and unblinking, and I hug him consolingly, tuck him down the front of my shirt so that his small-eared little head can peek out over the top. This is how Birdy herself ferries him around everywhere she goes—everywhere except fourth grade. He's like Mary's little lamb. I often wonder about the strangers grinning hugely at Birdy, and then I remember that they're seeing a cotton-candy-colored monkey head smiling at them over the neck of her T-shirt.

His name is Strawberry, and he's a floppy beanbag toy, the kind designed for a baby to clutch and chew and fling. Years ago, Birdy fell in love with him at a local tourist trap, in the candle-smelling corner of bless-this-mess kitchen plaques and overpriced toys. When we stop in now for cider or doughnuts,

CATHERINE NEWMAN

Birdy whispers to him, "This is where you were born!" Which is exactly what I whisper to her when we visit friends with new babies at our local hospital. I realize this is not a coincidence.

Strawberry is the soul of patience and adventure: he has gone camping and sailing, bowling and ice-skating, rock climbing and apple picking. He is, like Birdy, a vegetarian, a board-game fanatic, and a Democrat. He has seen *Ratatouille, Brave,* and *Toy Story 3* (which made him cry) from the back of our station wagon at the Wellfleet drive-in. He's been to three weddings and a bar mitzvah, tucked into Birdy's dress or suit jacket, depending on what kind of fancy she feels like. He has been grabbed up in the playful mouths of dogs and sniffed disgustedly by our cat. He has been barfed on at home and away, scrubbed out in our kitchen sink while Birdy shivered and cried, and under a hotel faucet while we apologized to the concierge and stripped the bed. He has been bathed in the plastic dolly tub and swaddled in a hand towel before getting powdered and sometimes, poor guy, diapered; he has spun through the gentle cycle countless times, and always emerges bright and smiling into Birdy's waiting arms. He has gamely worn a preemie onesie, a jaunty cap, a pair of doll overalls, a sleeveless wool dress cut from the sleeve of an old sweater, a cowl-neck cotton dress cut from a tube sock, and a homemade mermaid costume, complete with bottle-top bra. He trick-or-treats as a miniature version of Birdy: a flower fairy, with petaled skirt, tiny wings, and a wand taped to his willing arm; a robber, with a bandit mask, a loot bag, and the very face of innocence. He held his breath, alongside Birdy, inside that dark and noisy tunnel of the MRI machine. He smiles and smiles. He is utterly silent.

"I would totally want Strawberry to be alive," Birdy said recently. "But only if he could have his same personality."

He's like a pet, really—lavishly doted on and enthusiastically cherished, but unsullied by complicatedness or tantrums or the imperative to say *No thank you* instead of *Yucky eggy yuck.* Or by our expectations: Strawberry can grow up to be a wino, for all I care! Plus, he's adorable—this delicate primate alter ego—unlike some of the gross animals the kids attached themselves to over the years: the Pooh with its plastic nose and pilled nylon half-shirt; the blue souvenir bear with FLORIDA! embroidered across its chest; the various flea-market finds with their creepy stains and sewn-on trousers. The kids caught us once attempting a large seize-and-dump operation, a garbage bag full of the least loved of the stuffies—unfavorites we'd imagined, incorrectly, that we could sneak off to the Goodwill. "It's all the ones you guys don't even like!" we tried to explain. "The dinosaur puppet that gives you 'a weird feeling' and the dog with the 'creepy-sad face'!" Our children—and these were not *little* children, mind you—wept for their forsaken animals. "If we promise to love them more, can we keep them?" My god, what can you do?

But there's something darker about Strawberry, and I don't quite know how to put it into words. It's not that the Birdy smell of him makes my heart ache unspecifically, although it does. It's not that I project my love for her onto him, although that's getting at it. It's that somehow I project my *dread* onto him—my fear that she could be lost to us. One weekend last winter, Strawberry went missing and turned up only after a heroic search on the street next to her school. *Turned up* is not quite the right expression: Michael wandered the dark with a headlamp until he found Strawberry, who lay in a ditch, encased in ice, from which Michael hacked him out with an actual ax. Birdy clutched her smiling, frozen monkey and cried with relief. The next day brought two feet of fresh snowfall, and if we hadn't found him when we did, we never would have. I remember this detail because that was the same snowstorm that buried the lifeless body of a friend's son, dead in a freak skiing accident. *Thank god they got to him when they did,* everybody said. *Otherwise they wouldn't have found his body until spring.* That is the coldest comfort I have ever heard of.

Maybe it's totemic: *Let it happen to Strawberry.* Whatever it is. *Isn't this a nice monkey?* I send my thoughts to the gods, to any force that might listen. *Take him.* It's like the people we saw in Thailand, with their spirit houses—a tiny replica of their home, enticingly nicer than the big one, to trap the picky evil spirits who are more into luxury details than size. Instead, there's Strawberry. *Nothing to see here, folks! Just a toy monkey! Move along!* Although if anything happened to him, Birdy's sadness alone might kill me. And still, I picture punishment. I picture wringing my hands at a hospital bedside; I picture standing graveside; I picture myself bereft, Strawberry's mild face slicing me clean through with the razor, the rapture of grief.

After the ice incident, I scoured eBay for a spare Strawberry, a backup. Could Birdy learn to love another pink monkey? I really don't know. When I was pregnant with her, I was so devoted to Ben that the idea of loving another baby seemed vaguely grotesque. It made excellent sense to *have* another baby, of course, but only so we could harvest its organs in case Ben ever needed them. And then, oh, that fuzzy perfection of head, that valentine of face, that intoxication of lashes, of coal-dark eyes! I was doomed. We'd have to have a third if we wanted spare organs for the first two.

Birdy gets a fever and lies around unhappily, Strawberry tucked into her palely striped nightgown. When the phone rings, as if cued by my own fretfulness, it's the town itself, robocalling to tell us that there's an Eastern equine encephalitis high alert. Symptoms include fever and lethargy; it is nearly always fatal. While we listen to the message, I raise my eyebrows at Michael, and he shakes his head, pats my crazy shoulder. I am tempted to Google "too sick to even want a Popsicle Eastern equine encephalitis." But I don't.

The thing is, of course, we lose them metaphorically all the time. Their little selves are swallowed up by their bigger selves, and they're all nested in there, I know. They disappear and reappear, all those versions. They toddle away and back. They stretch and return, shrug you off and then crawl into your lap. At some point the big kids lose so many teeth that you catch a flash of their old gummy baby smiles—the ones that turn your heart into a staggering clubfoot. This is the kind of loss that's actually called *growth,* and we're lucky for it. But one day it's going to be totally *Velveteen Rabbit* around here: Strawberry in a box with the rest of the castoffs. One day, I will find him and cry. And he will mean *Birdy*, still and always, the face of sweet and blameless perfection. He is a metaphor, a symbol, an appendage, an extension, a projection, a fact. He is a transitional object. He is an object of devotion. He is hers, as she is—not quite, not ever truly—mine.

How to Not Have a Baby

I am having my blood drawn for the third time in four days. "Me again!" I say to the cute hoop-earringed phlebotomist. He smiles and then looks politely away while tears leak out of my eyes and into my hair. I'm sure he's not supposed to talk to me about my *situation,* but when I stand up to go, he punches me gently on the arm he hasn't stuck and smile-frowns. He says, "Hey, I hope this turns out good for you." My chart says *Pregnancy. Suspected ectopic.* As I leave, he's swabbing the chair with alcohol, and I feel contagious.

If you've had one go badly, then you know the terrible exponential math at the beginning of a pregnancy. Hormone levels are supposed to double every three days, and you picture these numbers as a representation of the baby itself: it's getting twice as big, twice as big again, cells properly multiplying in a kind of magical embryological choreography. Everything folds up the way it should. A flat plane of cells becomes tubes and tunnels, because your body has learned origami while you were sleeping! You are so good at this! Multiplication is your best and favorite function! But not always. Sometimes the numbers go down instead of up, a simple subtraction problem represented by the kind of dark blot in your underpants that makes you sit there with your head in your hands long after you're done peeing. That was the kind of miscarriage I had before Ben, and it was quick and certain. After a second trip to the clinic down the street, a friend who happened to work there walked over with our results. She hugged me. "Not this one," she said. "But it will happen." And it did. But first this melancholy reproductive subplot had to end, what with the bleeding and the cramping and my drama queen of a body throwing its miserable clots into the toilet.

This time there is no clarity, of either multiplication or subtraction. This pregnancy stays in a kind of algebraic twilight zone: $x = x = ?$ Nobody knows. At first I picture a stalled-out ball of cells, neither growing nor dying. In nine months I will birth our beautiful blastocyst! I will swaddle it tenderly and push it around proudly in a pram. Babies with limbs and facial features? "Totally overrated!" I'll say. "This one's so easy!" I say this jokily to a friend and she tortures me by not laughing. I am left hanging in more ways than I can count.

The stalling continues, my doctor goes on vacation, and her substitute is suspicious. If you might have one, don't Google "ectopic pregnancy." You will picture not only your baby growing uncomfortably in your fallopian tube—"Mama! I'm too squashed!"—but also your own death, your motherless children and motherless blastocyst clothed for school by a man who can't remember if it's a *skirt* or a *dress* that "also has the shirt part." Blood work, numbers, no change. Day after day.

I am superstitious enough that I worry about the wish I make every year when I blow out my birthday candles: *let everything stay the same*. What kind of wish is that? It's a crazy wish! I'm like Midas, only instead of a daughter made of gold I'm going to permanently have a three- and six-year-old, along with this ball of cells. Fifty years from now, I am going to be so sick of these ages. "Why can't you be more like the ball of cells?" I'll say to Ben and Birdy. "You don't hear *it* arguing about the compost smell!" I always thought this wish was an improvement over my childhood wish—that I not have seen the terrifying Injun Joe cave scene in the *Tom Sawyer* movie—but now I'm not so sure.

I had not pictured being an adult as the crazy derangement of joy and sadness that it's turning out to be. The children, for example, are lost to us over and over again, their baby selves smiling at us from photo albums like melancholy little ghosts of parenthood past. Where are those babies? They are here and not here. I want to remember the feel of a warm little hand in mine, or the damp, silky weight of a naked kid in my arms straight from the bath. When I prop Birdy on my hip, she still slings a little arm around my shoulder, jaunty as a boyfriend— but she's so heavy. The kids grow and grow, they grow right out the door! Like creatures in a Dr. Seuss book about people you love and love and then they move out and leave you and go to college like jerks, marry other people, and refuse to live at home with you who love them so much, who loved them first. (Assuming you can even keep them alive that long.) Loss is ahead of us, behind us, woven into the very fabric of our happiness. I don't wish nothing would change as much as I wish for the absence of more loss.

This, now, is change *and* loss. We didn't even want a third child. I will give you a secret piece of advice. Ready? If you are ever kneeling above me with a wrapped condom in your hand and I say, panting, "No, no, we're good, it's safe"? We're *not* good, and it's *not* safe. Just, you know, FYI.

Birdy is three and Ben is six, and I don't want another baby. I fear change, for one thing (see above), and for another I am starting to be not tired, which is intoxicating. The problem is that, also, I *do* want another baby. I have always loved to get pregnant, by accident or on purpose, in a way that I can't really describe or explain. I don't mean that I always knew I wanted to have kids, although that's true too. I mean that since I've been having sex, I have always, and sometimes secretly, hoped to get pregnant from having it, even at times in my life when I fervently didn't want to get pregnant. This is as crazy as it sounds. After some poorly contracepted sex with my high school boyfriend, I was terrified that I might be pregnant. And by *terrified* I mean something more like *tantalized*. It would have totally screwed up my track season, but I wanted to be pregnant anyway. The excitement is definitely part of it— the reproductive equivalent of a bee buzzing against your classroom windows, and everyone screaming or running out of the room. A break in the routine! Something fabulously different from American history, even if you end up getting stung! I got my period, between classes, in the third-floor bathroom with the big silver radiator that never turned off, even when it was broiling out. "Phew," I said from my stall, sweating, to my best friend. "A total relief." And this was and wasn't true.

It is not new to me, ambivalence, and the pregnancy desire has not always matched desire itself: I have gotten pregnant with a bonfire raging in my heart, and I have also gotten pregnant with the matter-of-factness of boiling an egg or tripping over the flipped-up corner of the doormat. I have gotten pregnant using birth control well, using it badly, and using it not at all. Which is, you'll notice, more pregnancies than the number of children I have. And yet every time, I have thrilled to the peed-on plastic stick with its baffling system of symbols: plus, minus, yea, nay. I always want to be pregnant. And even the losses have satisfied an odd craving, like a hook on which I've hung the heap of despair piled up inexplicably on the floor of my psyche. I don't always understand my own sadness. Me and my Achilles heart.

Did you see the final episode of *M*A*S*H*? Do you remember Hawkeye and his flashback about a woman choking a chicken to death because it was making too much noise on the bus and they feared for their lives? Only then the memory came into focus, and it wasn't a chicken, it was a baby? In this story, mine, the miscarriage comes into focus, and it's actually an abortion. Only it's not this miscarriage, it's an earlier one, which left behind the same agony of emptiness. But that's not the story I'm choosing to tell you here, although it's part of this story, the same way old bones are part of the milk in your baby's cup.

After the red ectopic herring, the numbers drop to zero and turn this into, yes, a plain old miscarriage. Uncertain as I am about the baby, I will be bereaved by its goneness. I will be alone, drinking the bitter reproductive blend of privacy and shame. "You have to remember to ask me about it every day," I will cry to Michael, whose body will not offer him gory reminders of the wreckage. Later that week, Ben will crawl into bed with us after a nightmare, and moments after Michael whispers, "Tell us all about it, sweetie," we will hear him gently snoring—which will make Ben and me laugh, but will also make me want to kill him. I will be furious. I will be depressed. Everybody around me will be suddenly hugely pregnant, tee-tering around on little feet like circus performers. I will take a lot of baths. I will buy a lot of maxi pads. I will kneel on the floor to fish a dark shape out of the toilet, then scrub my hands before touching my living, right-here children. The would-be baby will fade into a melancholy background hum, a kind of pale outline that fills in on its due date, on its birthday a year after that. We will try again, but without conviction. I will start to feel old, to doubt my ability to bear anything other than a phlegmy little clump of cells, to doubt I have the energy to rock the clump to sleep every night.

On medical forms, I will write a number for "pregnancies" and a number for "live births," and they will not be the same number. I will be indignant. "Live births? Are we guppies?" Eventually, I will be almost entirely happy again, under only the faintest shadow of doubt. Birdy will tell us that she remembers when they took Ben out of my belly. "I was already there, and they saw me there, and they took Benny out, and they closed you back up!" she'll explain. "I had to wait." "You were so, so patient," I'll say, and she'll nod smugly and shrug. "I was."

How to Quit Babies

In the backseat of the car, the baby is crying. Like most babies, he quiets down a little when we're moving, then starts up again when we hit a red light. Instead of coming to a full stop, I jerk the car back and forth—accelerator to brake—hoping to jiggle him from his misery, just as I did with the two babies before him.

The fact that this particular baby is feline rather than human is turning out to be a surprisingly minor detail, like a new china pattern, but hey, it's still a plate. I am filled with dotty, nearly heartbreaking devotion and, also, something like despair. *What have we done?* I think, just as I did when Ben was born, and then again when Birdy came along after. *Life was sailing along so nicely—why did we rock the boat?* At night, the kitten sleeps on my chest with his whiskery face pressed into my neck and his needly little claws kneading the tender skin there. If I try to dislodge him, he whimpers pitifully, and I can only imagine how bereft he feels—missing his cat mom and the furry heap of brothers and sisters—and so I let him stay. He purrs if I cough or sneeze. He purrs if I whisper in his ear or stroke his cheek or scratch under his chin. He purrs and purrs like a tractor engine, and come daylight, I am exhausted. But his paws smell like corn chips, his ears are as big as satellite dishes, and he is our baby.

"They sleep most of the time," everyone had said about the babies—and this was true but also not true. The cumulative hours of awakeness were not long, but they were surreally packed with many lifetimes of nursing and spitting up and pooping and crying. And here we are again: the kitten is like the corny calendar pictures of a kitten—a gentle ball of fur asleep in a basket, on the couch, in a salad bowl, inside a shopping bag. So how he finds time to eat all the plants and poop on the kids' wizard hat and shred a bag of bagels is a mystery. But there is no turning back. We are exhausted and also sick with love. Plus, he brings out, in the kids, something like the opposite of sibling rivalry: they love him as much as we do, and love each other more for the shared experience of devotion. They lie on the bed to watch him sleep, and every time he stirs, there's a collective chorus of squealing admiration. "Oh, did you see him *yawn?*" "He's *breathing* so cutely!" "Did you hear that little *snore?*" It reminds me of the videos we made of our one-week-old Ben, grunting and inert on his changing table. When he bats once at his mobile, you hear me whisper to Michael, "Oh my god—did you get that on film?"

At night the kitten gets what we call "the bedtime crazies"

and tears around the house like a maniac, careening into chair legs, his claws scrabbling against the hardwood. He cries over his shots at the vet, and I say consolingly, as I have said so many times before, "Poor, poor baby." He falls down the stairs and chokes on his food and nods off while he's playing, a felt mouse still clasped in his fierce, sleeping jaws. He tumbles into the bathtub, pees on the carpet, and chews an elaborate pattern of teeth marks into my leather belt. And how I feel is *healed*.

I have two children and too many blessings to count, and yet I have longed for one last cottony little baby to hold. I didn't always—two had seemed like plenty. But then there was that unplanned pregnancy that ended almost before it started: a moment of a two-lined stick, then three or four days of breathless, startled expectation that left, in its small wake, a vast longing. Afterward, my obstetrician showed me the ultrasound image of my uterus, collapsed on the floor of my pelvis like a deflated party balloon. "I'm not saying you couldn't try again," she said, but I felt old already. I didn't want to start all over again. At least not exactly.

I didn't imagine that a kitten would pull me through the last dregs of this unexpected grief, but that's what happened. He is a baby, plain and simple: he sleeps on my chest and I am trapped and happy beneath him, woozy with love. His breath reminds me of Birdy's milky exhalations. His fragrantly licked fur reminds me of the spitty smell of Ben's sucked thumb. I think about my parents getting a dog when their last baby— me—left for college, and I understand it now, even though my nest is far from empty. But a pet fills a hole perfectly. We don't care if he's smart. He will never grow up and leave us or even, really, grow up at all. He will die, yes; as Carol Anshaw puts it in one dog-lovers' novel, "Taking on a pet is a contract with sorrow." But that's sorrow for a later day. For now, there is an absence of sorrow. In fact, the kitten rolls on his back to get his belly rubbed, he closes his eyes, and my own fill with tears of what you might call joy.

How to Be Doomed

Ben and Birdy are sick. They are home from school, both of them dozing feverishly with their weirdly crimson cheeks, their dark crescents of eyelashes. You'd think, given the scares we've had, that I wouldn't worry so much about the everyday viruses. But I do. I still do. Because I've read about people losing their kids to common childhood illnesses—one minute someone's getting a strep test, the next minute their organs are failing in an ICU. And I almost believe that if I look this fact in the eye every day, if I remember that it could be us, that we could lose everything, then I can ward it off. I believe this is called magical thinking. Or preemptive grief. Or insanity.

I worry, when I'm most happy, that my very happiness is a paradoxical symptom of imminent disaster, and I blame popular culture. Joy-turned-catastrophe is a favorite trope: the way you're yanking the AMITYVILLE: SOLD! sign from your lovely lawn only moments before being paranormally assaulted. Or the way the happiest couple on a hospital TV show are doomed to lose that baby they're so buoyantly expecting. Or the way it's always the laughing soldier with the prettiest photo of his wife who'll die first in a war movie, the most angelic child in the world who will fall gravely ill. Bad things really do happen, of course, and they seem most tragic in the context of happiness, loveliness, joy.

My brother, the doctor, once explained to me—a migraine sufferer—that a feeling of euphoria often precedes a migraine. *Thanks for letting me know.* Now every time I'm happy I have to wonder if I'm about to get the worst headache of my life. It's like this Beth Ann Fennelly poem, "The Gods Watch Us Through the Window":

We sit at the table with the fourth side open,
the perfect family show. Claire belts "Twinkle, Twinkle,"
How I wa wa *(mumble)* are!
We beam like stars. Isn't she gifted? Isn't life great?

What a large target we make.
The great dramas all begin like this:
a surfeit of happiness, a glass-smooth pond
just begging for a stone.

It's not that I never worried before I had kids, it's that my worries had an everyday quality to them ("I hope nobody steals our car!") rather than the apocalyptic, death-and-mayhem catalog of possibilities that arrives daily in the in-box of my brain.

It's not just me, I know. Thinking about my sorry state, I put a kind of misery-loves-company query out on Facebook—*What kinds of crazy stuff have you guys worried about as parents?*—and I am sucked under a tidal wave of worries. No fewer than fifty friends message me with anxieties that include, but are not limited to: abduction; food dyes; television; a babysitter who talked to the kids about reincarnation; the baby falling down the stairs, falling out the window, falling off a bridge, falling from Ireland's Cliffs of Moher; acne; drug addiction; "two words: raw chicken"; early-onset puberty; swollen lymph glands; a blinky tic thing someone's daughter started doing last year; clubfeet; food allergies; unhappiness; reflux; and, of course, whether or not the baby's still breathing at night, in the sling, and when her neck looks all bent like that in her car seat.

I am no longer the newly minted mother of twelve years ago, the one who couldn't walk down a flight of stairs without picturing the baby falling from my arms and tumbling to his death, the one who couldn't cross a street without summoning the imaginary bus to mow us over. But I still suffer from the kind of worry that makes you Google "fatal rash" and assume the worst, assume the craziest, assume they're going to die while you wring your useless hands and poison ivy morphs bubonically.

Around the world, women behave like normal, rational people—and then they have children and become maternal tornadoes of fretting and panic. Turkish mothers, I have heard, will pin blue-glass *nazar* amulets to their children to ward off the evil eye. Farther east, the Hmong have a practice of putting their children in colorful hats so that the evil spirits looking down will mistake them for flowers and leave them alone. I feel the same way. I would wreathe my children's fragile necks in climbing ivy, cover their hair with pom-poms, scent them with blossoms, if I thought it would protect them—and if they wouldn't have to, you know, go to school with the ivy and pom-poms and be mad at me all day. Instead, I live in anticipation of my own broken heart, and I'm trying to learn how to move through the world like that, with fears fluttering after me like streamers. I'm trying to believe that I won't be punished for my happiness—that we aren't jinxed by the very fact of our healthy, joyful lives.

Time helps; it does. As the kids get older, their durability seems somehow likelier. I'm less stricken. Even now, I marvel at the astonishing rise and fall of their breath. They mutter and wake, sip ginger tea with honey, and allow their cooling foreheads to be kissed. That's it. I can't inoculate myself against heartbreak by worrying. The point, all over again and always, isn't that nothing bad could happen—it's that we're so lucky to have so much to lose.

How to Be Intrepid

"Hibernaculum," Birdy says again, patiently, after I shake my head at the word. "It's a place where all the snakes are waking up." *All the snakes* is not a phrase I'm in love with. Especially followed by *waking up*. I must shudder visibly, because Birdy laughs. "I know!" she says, and pats me. "It sounds so terrible! I thought the same thing. And it is. But it's amazing."

Because this hibernaculum, to which a teacher has taken her class, is within walking distance of our house, the four of us set off through the woods. It's early spring, some scraps of ground thawing darkly, some still patchy with ice. We will experience this cold-blooded waking nightmare ourselves in just a minute—but still we pepper Birdy with questions. *How many snakes are there?* "Fifteen?" she says, making a little *más-o-menos* sign with her hand. "Maybe fifty? I'm not so great at estimating." *What are they doing?* She shrugs. "Just, kind of, *being snakes.*"

I picture the asp-infested Well of Souls from *Indiana Jones and the Raiders of the Lost Ark*. I picture the basilisk from *Harry Potter and the Chamber of Secrets*. I picture, crystal clear, the spitting cobra from my early childhood viewing of *Born Free*, although the lions and humans have all faded to sepia.

We are a snake-fearing family. We are afraid of Kaa, the loopy cartoon snake in *The Jungle Book*. We are afraid of those hinged wooden toys that slither and snap with alarming realism, and of those prank boxes in which a pulled-open lid causes the darting of a forked-tongue viper. (I am even afraid of the speckled coils that spring from joke peanut cans, although that's just me.) Our collective knees go weak in any reptile house, in any zoo, although we share a particular horror over the signs at the one in the Bronx: PLEASE DON'T TAP ON THE GLASS. WHAT WOULD YOU DO IF IT BROKE? ("Um, drop dead of fright, I'm thinking?" Ben answers.) We dream often about snakes and share our dreams—"And then Mama had a snake in her lap? And it was *furry!*"—scaring one another to pieces and making me revisit my thinking on Freud and psychoanalysis. "Would you rather see an exceptionally long and skinny snake or a short one that was super thick?" we ask one another, and debate the relative terror of each. We relish our fear, linger delightedly over it. We're afraid of the snakes in the woods, in my parents' garage, in an awful black tangle on the bike path, the glossy surprise of slither and coil. We don't want to go to the Everglades, but we *kind of* want to read about the python epidemic there—pythons eating crocodiles who've eaten babies, like the terrifying reptile version of a turducken.

This is the same *kind of* that defines the family feeling about Snakey, our backyard's resident garter who returns every May to sun himself in the parsley, coiled blackly, before disappearing again after a month or two. He was a baby the first time he showed up—six or seven inches long at most, and slim as a pencil—which did not stop us from screaming and screaming and laughing behind the safety of our door's glass. Now he is a full-grown snake, thick as a bike tire, and we speak to him with nervous but genuine affection, afraid and happy that he has returned to us. "As long as I know where he is," Birdy explains, capturing the feeling we all share, "I like to see him. It's the surprise I can't really handle."

Which is what makes the hibernaculum so perfect for us. So perfectly therapeutic. "The snakes have their little ditch, and that's where they stay, which is kind of nice," Birdy is explaining. "It's not like walking in the woods and one squiggles in front of you suddenly." She's right. We arrive and, at first, don't even see anything—just a sunny trench on the side of the path. The ground is upholstered in wet brown leaves, interrupted by a low overhang with an opening beneath, like a cave for dollhouse people or fairies. Birdy beckons us to squat down, and even as we do, we are starting to see them: small and brown, five or six, with their necks stretched up, their little faces tipped toward the sun. "Do snakes have necks?" I whisper, and get promptly shushed. Because there aren't five or six; there are maybe a dozen. Or two dozen. The more you look, the more you see—snakes sliding in and out of the hole, sliding down from farther up the hill, up from down in the streambed, dozens of them. If you fix your eyes on any one snake, you will eventually see it lift its head, all of them perfectly synchronized, like a yoga class.

"I am shitting my pants," I whisper, but only to make the kids laugh—which they do—because I'm not actually afraid. I am awestruck.

Put the thing you fear in plain sight, where you can see it. Let your vague dread gather itself up into an arrow, pointing right at the worst thing. Then hang out awhile, looking at it. For Ben, this is the idea of drifting untethered through the blackness of space like a dot of imminent asphyxiation. "The only thing that scares me more than being adrift in space," he explains, "is being adrift at sea—alone in the waves. And that's only because it's more plausible. Plus," he adds, "sharks."

I'm finding most of my old fears faded to pale. Even the scariest movies of my youth—Hitchcock, *Poltergeist, Aliens*—provoke in me now a nearly complete absence of fear. Yes, the poltergeist opens up a giant throbbingly squashlike tunnel in the wall, sucks in the furniture, the kids even, but I shake my head. This will not happen to me. Some poor somebody's head pops off in *The Thing* and scuttles away upside down, an arachnid of decapitation, and I notice only the gore in its wake. "What a mess," I say abstractedly, as if it's a cleanup I'm adding to my to-do list. Even *The Shining* I see now for the mundane domestic horror story that it is: snowed in with a writer? That really *is* kind of scary. Only I'm not scared.

I am phobic about snakes, and I'm sure that if a black mamba—the single snake that will actually chase you—

actually chased me, I would drop preemptively dead. But the only thing I truly fear is that I will lose the children. A vast illuminated fog of worry, pre-kids—that our house would be broken into, that I'd break my leg Rollerblading, that I'd get the flu, lose my job, step in dog shit, eat a bad mussel—has contracted into this single, slicing laser of fear.

"What's up?" Michael will say, because I've inhaled audibly, and I say, "Nothing," before he can look over and see the palm spread over my beating, ruined heart—this heart that would like to, yet will never, steel itself. What can you answer, without sounding like the kind of person you'll see again only in a padded room? "Oh, nothing. I just for no reason pictured our daughter falling off the monkey bars and breaking her neck." "Me? Pfff. Just the odd image of our son dying in a hospital bed from the tumor we mistook for a bruise." I am afraid not only that they will die, but that they will be *afraid* and then die—and that I will need to comfort them. This is what I could not think about, could not stop thinking about, after 9/11: parents on the doomed planes with frightened children looking into their faces for reassurance. The fear coils in my chest. It happens all the time, all over the world—the parents who smooth a child's creased forehead and whisper "Angel"; the ones in war-crazed places, their injured babies wide-eyed and silent in their arms.

Once, we were crowded into an elevator and it stopped in between floors, the doors opening onto a brick wall. Both children looked up at me, alarmed, studying my eyes for clues. "We're safe," I smiled, even as I pictured plummet and free fall. Birdy, in that MRI tunnel, did not take her eyes off my face, her own a shifting collage of fear and trust. I squeezed her hand, winked at her, made soothing sounds while the crazies scrolled past like looped film: deathbed and coffin, a keening, endless grief.

They start when they're babies—looking to you to absorb your absence of concern, to mirror your trust. A big dog, a friendly stranger, a clap of thunder. *Am I okay? Am I? I am. I am.* I stifle my fear to stifle theirs. Here, though, it's easy. These are just babies—"They're somebody's snake babies!" Birdy actually announces—and, even snake-fearing me, I know they will do us no harm. I laugh and shake my head, point, amazed. My heartbeat quickens, sure, but it's as fake and fun as a roller coaster.

This is not looming doom or a miasma of dread. It's just little snakes, seeking some sunshine. And so when the kids look up into my eyes, I smile for real. I promise them safety. In this moment, at least. Which is all we've ever really got.

VII

BECOMING

How to Talk (and Talk) About Talking

Maybe it starts because we're already talking about language. "What does *frittata* even mean?" ten-year-old Birdy asks through a mouthful of it. I explain that it comes from the Italian word for *fried*, which does not seem to quite capture her sense of the word's staccato delight. It should be Italian for *eggs used as percussion instruments* or *eggs so good they make you stutter.* "Plus, it's kind of like a trick. *Fried* sounds like *French fries.* Not like a big, dry egg thingy. No offense." None taken.

Next up: genitalia. Segue: none discernible. "I kind of can't believe that *manhole* is something people actually say," Ben says. He is thirteen, and the strangeness of the world dawns on him afresh every day. "Like, *Oh, don't fall into that* manhole! *Don't worry, I won't—it's got a* manhole cover." He stops to chew, then adds, "There's kind of no getting around the condom-y sound of that." Indeed not. And if there's a better time than dinner to talk about the word *vagina*, my family hasn't found it. "It's just so weird-sounding!" Birdy announces, laughing. "Is it weird because of what it means? Or is it really just weird?"

"*Vagina* is actually the Latin word for *sheath*," I say, having taken no fewer than one hundred years of high school Latin. The kids grimace at this information. "What do you guys make of *that?*"

And what they make of that is a lot. We talk about how naming the vagina for *sheath* means that its main purpose is—by definition—to hold a sword. Which is a disturbingly violent image, on the one hand, and, on the other, gives the woman's body significance only in passive relationship to the man's. "If you named the woman's part *slot machine* and the man's part *coin,* at least it would give you a different sense of who was doing what," I say, confusingly, since (a) A slot machine doesn't actually work without the coin and (b) Now I picture a winning trio of cherries, quarters pouring from my own crotch. This is not an especially empowering image. "Is *penis* Latin for *sword?*" the kids want to know, sensibly enough—and it's not, but I explain that it's actually related to the word *pen.* Pen and sword are both pretty mighty and, by these early definitions, pretty much man tools.

"The word *vagina* makes it kind of hard to describe being a lesbian," Birdy muses. "Don't mind us—nothing to see here, folks—just two sheaths kind of *sheathing together.*" It's not how I would have explained the constraints of language to a classroom of feminist-theory students, but she's totally right.

Of course, it wasn't always like this, the dinnertime conversation. When Ben was newly born, I looked at our dinner table and saw only a good place to store diapers and butt ointment and the remaining fragments of my sanity. Who needs a dinner table when you can stand over the changing table with a piece of cold pizza in your hand, cranking and recranking Brahms's "Lullaby" to keep the baby distracted for the one minute it takes to chew and swallow? There were years of eating dinner while I bounced on an exercise ball with a baby in my arms, while somebody gulped noisily from the spigots of my person, while crumbs sprayed around the high chair like there might be hungry pigeons to feed, while a diapered somebody stood next to me, held on to my thigh, looked up into my face, and said, straining and tragic, "I pooping, Mama." "Yes, you are, sweetie!" *And I'm eating eggplant Parmesan.*

Back then I imagined that, at best, we would one day return to some approximation of the life we'd had before: dinnertime that involved some eating, some chatting, something more than five unbroken minutes at the table. I missed and craved the old luxuriously relaxed meals—meals that weren't dominated by my vigilance and anxiety as somebody toddled away from the table to go choke on a Tinkertoy and fall down the stairs. Or by my irritation as somebody rubbed sweet potato into her own head and then cried about it, accusatory, "Hair yucky!" Ten minutes was all I wanted. I wanted not to be the person walking the baby up and down the clam-shack parking lot while my scallop roll arrived, cooled, and congealed. And I had no idea what I was in for.

Because now they're turning into thinkers—the kind of people who want to talk about the fact that things are not always, and not simply, as they seem. Language is tricky, because we imagine that we control it but we don't. To speak is not to pull transparent meaning, godlike, from thin air; it's more like composing a mosaic from a bin of used tiles, and some of the tiles are dirty or broken or not really the color you wanted, or someone has written "bitch" on one in tiny letters. *What language is available to me?* I want the kids to ask themselves. *What meanings do words carry along with them, beyond the ones I intend?* Words have history, assumptions, even bigoted connotations that they drag along on their shoes like toilet paper, into your own speech and, even, your own thoughts.

"Sometimes words are the wrong tool for the job," I'm saying now, the frittata plates pushed away. "It's like getting a set of Lincoln Logs, only what you want to make is a spun-glass ornament. How do you say the thing you want to say if there aren't even the words to say it?"

Ben mentions the classic (debated) example of Eskimos having fifty words for *snow,* and we discuss the significance of that chilly linguistic abundance—how it both reflects, but also helps create, the cultural importance of snow. (I do have to interrupt the snow conversation to talk about the word *Eskimo* itself, and why it might be problematic for Aleutian, Inuit, and Yupik people—bringing racist history along for the ride, as it does, like an insidious little hitchhiker.) Knowing fifty words for *snow* allows you not just to *describe* fifty different kinds of snow, but to see them in the first place: the kind of snow that means spring is coming or the kind of snow that makes your eyelashes look sparkly (I'm just imagining here), whereas we're like the

oafs of winter precipitation, with our single grunting distinc-
tion between *snow* and *sleet*.

In English, we have to borrow *Schadenfreude* from the Ger-
mans because we have *joy* and we have *damage*, but, given
our love of keeping unlike things apart, we don't have a word
that contains both at the same time. Or related, but more
charged, there's the Native American word *berdache*, which
means *two-spirit*—a gender category that falls between *man*
and *woman* and knocks those words from their binary orbit.
I explain this to the kids. "Oh," Birdy says. "It's like *ze*, you
know, at Hampshire." Indeed, some students at a local college
have been agitating for a third gender designation besides *he*
or *she*—and for a bathroom to go with it. Long-haired Ben is
interested in this idea, despite the fact that he identifies fully
as a boy. "*Ze* means there aren't just two kinds of everybody,"
he says. "And it's true. There aren't." He smiles dazzlingly, his
cheeks like freckle-dotted plums, and I think *exactly*.

I'm reminded of the conversation we had a few weeks ago,
when a young friend had been over and we'd gotten out Guess
Who?, an old favorite board game of the kids'. Playing requires
a kind of process-of-elimination deduction—like the war game
Battleship, only instead of marine coordinates, Guess Who? is
based on offensive visual stereotypes. You have to guess the
other player's character by asking questions (Does your person
have long hair? Is your person black?) and then flipping down
all the characters you know it's not until you're left with the
right one. Ben was looking at the game like he'd never seen it
before. "You know what I just realized?" he said. "This game is,

like, practically all white men. Without even thinking about it, I've always been like, *I hope I don't get a woman or a black person or I'll be screwed!* How messed up is that?" Very! But he's right. If you get, say, the one black woman, the other player will be able to guess who you are right away. "White guys win," my son concludes, drily.

We watch the Summer Olympics and talk about the women gymnasts with their spingly-spangly eye makeup, still compelled to be decorative even at their most muscularly athletic. "They should make the men weightlifters wear glittery eye shadow too!" Birdy says, and we laugh to imagine it. We talk about *Beauty and the Beast,* Ben concluding that the implicit message is that it's your job, as a woman, to tame your violent boyfriend, and Birdy concluding that, thanks to the princely metamorphosis, the moral of a story that appears to be about acceptance is really *"Oh, phew, he's actually pretty."* (She uses the word *pretty* totally unself-consciously.) Am I making it sound like we order a pizza, then sit around reading aloud to one another from Umberto Eco, chuckling lightly? It's not like that. But beyond the simple, analytic pleasure of it, this kind of thinking is also, for me, the highest form of optimism: if you want a better life for everyone, then you need to see what's what— even the hidden things—so you can figure out what you need to change. That's not cynicism. It is eyes wide open, seeing the world as it really is, and also seeing, in the distance, a better one.

There are measurable benefits to dinner-table conversation. It's a natural check on overeating, for example. Even if you're talking and eating at the same time, you simply can't generate the same spaghetti-shoveling velocity that you could if you were eating silently. Plus, I'm sure it's good for mental health, for social health, for learning how to become a good date—although, my god, I'll miss them when there's someone they're dating besides us. It's a reminder too that I have to pay attention. Those conversations when the kids are trying to tell me something but I don't close my laptop long enough to look them in the eye and listen? Let me tell you how much I remember about those: nothing. But some of it is immeasurable too. What deep conversation gives us is time to stop and appreciate how much we have right now even as we imagine, deliriously, that it could go on forever.

The candles burn low, and the children are on to one of their other favorite topics: *What if you had to pick a really weird name?* Past contenders have included Poopy Diaper versus I Pooped My Pants or the Great Buttholio versus Arsewipe, but tonight they follow the theme. "If you *had* to be called it, and you *had* to tell people it was your name," Ben is saying, "and it was spelled *Vagina* either way, would you rather be named Va-*jean*-a or *Vah-zhee-nah?*" "I don't know," Birdy says, "but what if you could keep your name but then you'd have to get a picture of a vagina tattooed on your forehead instead?" I leave the table for bed because, clearly, my work here is done.

How to Express an Opinion

The kids have come into my bed, warm and fragrant from sleep, and we're lingering under the covers, even though it's a school morning. Early pink sunlight filters through the tiny octagonal window and sets our blue walls aglow. "I love our house," I say, and Birdy sighs from somewhere near my armpit and says, "Me too. So much." Ben is quiet—maybe he's asleep again. "I love our *doorknobs,*" I say. I can see three of them from here, and no two are the same: one is beautiful old cut glass, one is a dinged-up bronze, and the other looks the newest, a kind of fake vintage porcelain set into a brass plate. All of them predate us, like a knobby collage of other people's taste.

It's an old Cape, not ancient, but our bedroom ceilings are low and slanted, and there are traces of the decades of previous inhabitants: artifacts of disparate periods and styles that nobody has bothered, or wanted, to smooth over with coherence. The floors are all wood but appear to have been installed in different rooms during different decades, the maple boards here laid down this way even though the scuffed oak ones there are laid the other. There are newish cabinets in the kitchen, but nobody's done anything about the closets, of which there are three in the entire house, only one with a door, barely as deep as your arm. And then there are the doors themselves: most are thickly painted, with chips revealing colors layered like a Gobstopper, but the doors to the kids' tiny rooms are cut from barely finished pine, and they are so deeply luminous that someone must have thought them too beautiful to mar with knobs, which they don't have.

"Ugh. I *hate* our doorknobs." Ben is awake after all! Awake and filled with contempt! Who knew? "I think that might be the first time in your entire life that I've ever heard you use the word *hate*," I say, and Birdy laughs. "I was just thinking the same thing," she says. Ben is, typically, as pleasant and springy as a deep carpet of moss, and has been for his entire life. When he was three, he woke us once in the night, saying loudly from sleep, "I was still using that!" followed by the quieter, cheerful "Oh, okay, you go ahead, then." The worst thing I have ever heard him say about another person was in response to a recent question about a middle-school classmate: "Is she nice?" I'd asked, and he hesitated and said, barely tentative, "She is." "Oh, man," Birdy whispered to me, laughing. "She must be really awful."

"You hate the doorknobs," I say now, because I know about active listening, and Ben says again, "Ugh." And then "I hate the way they don't match. I wish they were all, I don't know,

187

brushed nickel or something." This is a kid who watches HGTV whenever there's cable, who droolingly studies the *New York Times* Great Homes and Destinations slideshows online and reads the IKEA catalog cover to cover like it's a book about a hero's journey through Swedish light fixtures to a better life. He is moved to exclamatory passion by such modernities as black flooring and vast white sectional sofas and open-concept steel staircases. I have suspected our scrappy Bohemian lifestyle and raggedy Salvation Army aesthetic of grating on him, but this is the first I've heard of it.

And, I'm embarrassed to admit, I bristle. I think: *Brat.* I say: "That's a couple hundred dollars I don't really want to spend on *doorknobs*. But you should feel free. Honestly, be my guest. You've got some money saved up. I'll drive you to Home Depot." "No, no," he says, mild again, and cowed. "It's stupid, I know. It doesn't matter." At which point I flush with shame. Because doorknobs don't matter, not really—but this lovely boy, trying to flex the new muscle of his differentness from us? That matters.

When they're little, and you're scraping them off your leg at a party so you can refill your wineglass and metabolically transform four or five pounds of cheese into the milk that's soaking through the front of your dress, you can't wait for the kids to become separate from you. Thanks to your mind, as open as a flower-dotted meadow, you know that you will rise to any occasion of individuality. You merrily indulge their clomping around in their rain boots for sunny months on end; you chuckle over their sudden quirky interest in Care Bears or jazz or chai. And you look to the future, imagining that you will be called upon to support your children's differentiation in ways that are delightful or noble or both: "I'm gay!" they will say, and you will rush to the streets in your PFLAG T-shirt, plaster your car with I GAILY SUPPORT MY GAY CHILDREN stickers. "I'm a vegetarian!" they will say, and you will stir-fry tofu happily, blanket it with nutritional yeast; you will adore the Buddhist boyfriend, you will donate to their bluegrass band's Kickstarter, and you will be pat-yourself-on-the-back perfect with the banjo-playing bacon-eschewing gay lotus-scented lifestyle your child has chosen.

Only that's not what it's like, because those things are only samenesses masquerading as difference. It's the actual differences, however tediously minute, that are truly challenging. What's hard about a child's differentiation is—*Aha* moment!—that it's *different* from you.

And what Ben wants to be is rich. He wants to live a white-and-black-and-silver life, climate-controlled and, ideally, featured in various aspirational publications. He is the proud owner of four shares of JetBlue stock, which he researched extensively before purchase. He prefers hotels to camping; he'd rather eat out than suffer another of my famous bean feasts; he likes nice ties and ties one on at the slightest provocation. He wants a poolside robot butler from Hammacher Schlemmer, despite our sore lacking of a pool or robot funds. In short, we have birthed Alex P. Keaton.

Do we press into him, like a kind of socialist steam iron, an understanding that profit tends to be carried to the wealthy on the backs of the working poor? Yes. Yes we do. And Ben wants to donate vast chunks of his future wealth to various worthy causes, writing enormous checks, à la Bill Gates, from the acre of mahogany desk on his own private island. Also, he has promised to take us on a private cruise of the Caribbean, an idea I confess to finding not unappealing, even if my Lilly Pulitzer cover-up will have been salvaged from the Goodwill.

Meanwhile, this kid just hates the doorknobs. Or— lightbulb!—wants one of his own? "Do you want a knob on your bedroom door?" I ask now. "It's honestly never occurred to me." "Oh, I'd love that," he says. "I'm kind of sick of not being able to close my door all the way." Our teenager. *Have you ever heard of privacy?* you are wondering. I know. Man, we are the lamest.

After school, we troll the aisles of Home Depot, and Ben carefully deliberates before picking out a brushed-nickel door-knob—one that locks, even. "Is that really okay?" he asks (like Oliver from *Oliver!*) and leans against me happily as I pay. I am thinking of long-ago fireworks—a film clip that plays in slo-mo of the children turning, terrified, and running into my open arms, tumbling, laughing, against me, and then running off again. A door is closing. It's a metaphor and, also, it's just the door—closing and opening, as doors do.

How to Be a Boy

One minute I am buttering a piece of baguette in the lodge, thinking that if I have to stuff my feet back into my ski boots I'll kill myself, and the next minute a man is standing red-faced before me, pointing at Ben and sputtering. "She was in the men's room! Your daughter was in the men's room! A girl in the men's room!" Alas, Ben's calm correction—"I'm a boy"—does nothing to mitigate this person's certainty that long hair only and always equals *girl*. He actually spittles on me with rage. I wipe my cheek, furious and afraid in equal measure.

Birdy cut her hair boy-short a month ago. Until then, though, everybody commented on the beauty of my daughters. Partly this is because Ben's hair, which he has not cut in three years, falls in a cape around his shoulders. And partly this is because he really *is* beautiful: as pink-cheeked and freckle-sprinkled as a frosted cupcake. He has not yet grown what we like to call, shudderingly, the bar mitzvah mustache. Plus, he wears a lot of pink clothing: nothing frilly or ruffly, but plenty of magenta velour hoodies and slim raspberry-colored T-shirts top his super-skinny jeans. Also, the bottom half of that very long hair is fuchsia. He dresses like this to make a very important statement. And that statement is *I like the color pink.*

But, of course, his benign stylistic preference has turned him into a de facto gender revolutionary. I had written "utterly meaningless stylistic preference," only it's not, not really. It *would* be meaningless, but only if it weren't so saturated with meaning. *If we can't tell if you're a boy or a girl, then how do we know if you need the vagina kind of prom date or the penis kind? How do we know you won't suddenly be starring in your own personal re-make of* The Crying Game—*some poor guy going openmouthed in horror while your skirt falls off to reveal a willy situation?* Behold the apocalypse! Wake me when it's over.

It's not that there aren't battles to pick—even ones about, yes, personal style. I feel like kids should go to school in clean clothes, with tidy hair that is not hanging over their eyes in a belligerent curtain. ("What if your teacher came in with muddy sweatpants and a balaclava pulled down over her face?" is the kind of rhetorical eye-roller I like to ask.) And if someone wanted to get a tattoo of, say, a swastika, I'd definitely put my foot down. But in terms of basic creative self-expression, it seems best to cultivate a kind of doting neglect—the type that gives the kids room to stretch and thrive and perform the latest version of themselves, even though, sure, it is tempting to train them to be ambassadors of my own good taste. Unmatched socks? Plaid worn with polka dots? This or that superhero cape or hairstyle or pair of rain boots? Whatever. Even if, yes, it's the tomato-red polo shirt—like a golfing parody from *Caddyshack*—that Birdy wears and wears until the day she sees a photo of herself in it and says, comically grimacing, "So *that's* what that shirt looks like. Good to know."

I know that gender adds to this benign costuming scenario something like a loaded gun, and that there is actual danger here. In fact, despite how badly I will miss that dewy, angelic face, I've found myself rooting for Ben to grow a beard, an Adam's apple, a jaw, a brow ridge, just so he won't get so much shit in the men's room. Because he gets a lot of shit in the men's room—from men who seem to imagine that a teenage girl would wander in on purpose to ogle a row of urinating guys. *(You wish.)* "You're in the wrong bathroom" is the temperate version of gender correction people try to foist on him. But the ski-lodge guy's is the menacing version. "Are you its mom?" he asks me, and I'm stunned. "His. He's a boy," I say, rising out of my chair to show him my claws and canines, my bristling fur, all eight feet of my ferocious height. "Still, still," the guy stammers. "Even if that's true. It shouldn't have been in there."

It's depressing, the way people don't seize on the experience of wonder as an opportunity for growth and learning. *That doll has short hair and is lying next to a pair of scissors. Did Ken's boobs get really big all of a sudden, or could there be another explanation? Or I wonder if that's a boy or a girl. The fact that this person is here in the men's room and seems comfortable might give me a clue.* If you found a darker *O* in your bowl of Cheerios, even though it didn't look exactly like the rest of your cereal, you might be able to deduce something about overbaking before you, say, freaked out that it was a wheel from the landing gear of a miniature UFO that was going to abduct you.

Ben is so, for want of a better word, cool at the ski lodge that I am filled with a kind of awed pride: *Who is this brave and beautiful person?* We will even laugh later, once the adrenaline has released our pounding hearts. Ben will imitate my larger-than-life mama-bear stance, and we will crack up about the guy's strange utterance: "I was naked in there! She saw me naked!" Ben: "I *would* have looked at your penis if it wasn't too small to see." We will imagine the solution of silk-screening an image of Ben's boy junk onto all of his clothes, and that will make us laugh too. But it also scares me, the fact—or the reminder—that gender nonconformity can trigger rage rather than pleasure or, even, confused curiosity. The thought "I don't know what you are" seems sometimes, dangerously, to be followed by the resolution "And so I hate you."

Even when Ben was a mere wisp of a newborn, boyness was like a peculiar blue shadow cast over him rather than anything that belonged properly to his baby self. Our best friends had had a baby before us, and Ben wore her hand-me-down onesies and rompers, all of them decorated variously with whimsical fruits and zoo animals. Nothing was frilly or girly or even *pink*, but because these were not typical boy-baby clothes—insofar as they were without the obligatory decals of footballs and bulldozers and naked women—Ben was often mistaken for a girl. Which was fine with us. I mean, it wasn't like we needed him to hop up and carve our Thanksgiving turkey or anything. He was only fifteen seconds old, after all. But people would gush over him—"Oh, what a pretty baby! Oh, she's gorgeous"—and we would beam and nod until the moment they asked "her" name, when we would have to confess, "Well, actually, it's Ben." And then his admirer would always fall into fits of apology. "Oh my god! I'm so sorry! I don't know how I missed it! I mean, now that I really look—he's so handsome. So *manly*." Even though little Ben would just be dozing neutrally in the front pack, with his rosebud lips and male-pattern baldness. It wasn't like he was cruising for a fiancé.

When Ben's favorite color turned out to be pink, there was more concern from the general public, and it always baffled me. Was the worry that pink would keep Ben from achieving his proper patriarchal birthright? *O masculinity! So natural and true! As teetering and precarious as an ice-fishing house built from fairy wings!* Will they uncover Ben's preschool class photo one day—our three-year-old smiling in his pinkly striped T-shirt—and forbid him to enter the World Wrestling Federation? Will those pink-threaded boyhood outfits prevent him from registering a firearm or sucking beer out of somebody's ass crack at a fraternity hazing? Will he be clinically incapable of slouching in front of the Super Bowl like an overgrown, chili-fed larva? Or do people just worry that he won't know how to camouflage himself properly as an *imbecile stone* when a lover tries to enter together with him, one day, into the world of human feelings? I mean, men are great and everything, but the last time I checked, gender roles didn't seem to be working so well for everyone. Why would we take such good care of something that seems to make so many people—gay and straight, men and women—so unhappy?

"Oh, that's okay," we always said when people mistook little Ben for a girl. "We don't care!" And we didn't. Or at least not about that. Because we *do* care—so much it's like an ache at the bottom of my throat—about other things. Like Ben's happiness. His wholeness.

But if you hurt them in the interest of preventing them from getting hurt—*You can't wear that because everyone's going to think you're weird (or gay)*—well, where's the sense in that? It seems like we should be teaching our kids not to judge other people based on how they look. Not to think they know everything based on what they can see. Not to care what people think, when that thinking is based on stereotypes rather than on, say, kindness. Would I choose for Birdy to wear her rainbow-yarn finger-knitted headband like she's in a biopic about Pat Benatar? Actually that's a bad example, because I would. Even though I might not pick the Lithuanian flag T-shirt worn over a white button-down Oxford, but so be it. Kids rarely get to be self-determining. It seems like the least we can do for them is let them decide how they want to look as they move, in various constrained ways, through the world.

Plus, we want them to be resilient and good-natured and sure of themselves. "Oh, it's fine," Ben reassures the people who are mortified over mistaking him for a girl. "Believe me, if I cared, I'd cut my hair." The reactions to his appearance are giving Ben the balls to deal with just about everything that comes his way, it turns out. And as far as ironies go, I like it.

How to Be a Girl

Birdy and her friend Keating have determined that "The Ali Mountain Song," a traditional tune they're singing as part of their China study, is sexist. "Ali Mountain girls are so very *lovely*," they sing for me, emphasizing each adjective in case I might be missing the object of their scorn. "Ali Mountain boys are very, very *strong*." They are outraged! They are plotting an intervention. I am in love with them. "I support your radical politics," I say, "but I wonder if you should try having a conversation with your music teacher before staging the whole shirt intervention." The shirt intervention involves silk-screening the word *strong* on Birdy's tee and the word *lovely* on Keating's, and then they'll unzip their sweatshirts in the middle of the performance and fling them off to reveal their extremist sensibilities like the radical little mutineers they are. I love their idea, I do, but I force myself to argue against it as a first-line response. "Give your music teacher a chance to be a friend before you make her into an enemy," I tell them. "If she doesn't respond in a way that works for you, then I'll help with the T-shirts."

Birdy is ten, and she's not nice, not exactly. She is deeply kind, profoundly compassionate, and, probably, the most ethical person I know, but she will not smile at you unless either she is genuinely glad to see you or you're telling her a joke that has something to do with butts or poop in the punch line.

Kids, it should be clarified, are an exception. Birdy is always nice to other children.

In this—her guarded approach to friendliness—Birdy is different from me. Sure, I spent the first half of the nineties wearing a thrift-store suede jacket that I'd accessorized with a neon-green FUCK THE PATRIARCHY! sticker plastered to its back. But even then I smiled at everyone! Because I wanted *everyone* to like me! *Everyone!* Friendly little political badass that I was. And am, still. Even now I put out indiscriminately, hoping to please not only our cherished friends and family, but also my son's orthodontist, the barista who rolls his eyes while I fumble apologetically through my wallet, the ex-boyfriend who cheated on me, and the Craigslist person who's overcharging me for her used cross-country skis. At the chicken-wing restaurant, it is important that I be our favorite waitress's favorite customer. I don't want good service: I want to be loved best of all. "How is everything, you guys?" Even if the celery looks like it's been used to scrub out a rusty drain hole, I say, "Everything's great! It's perfect!" I look over jealously when she's helping other people. I wonder if she'd love us more if we got those really huge beers that come in the samovar thing instead of just this regular urn of beer with a handle.

If I had all that energy returned to me—all the hours and neurochemicals and facial musculature I've expended in my wanton pursuit of likedness—I could propel myself to Mars and back. Or, at the very least, write the book *Mars and Back: Wasted Smiling.*

I understand that it's not one thing or another, of course. Friendliness tends to put people at ease—loved ones, neighbors, waitresses—which is a good thing. Plus, according to all those studies about self-fulfilling emotional prophecies, smiling probably makes me feel happier. I know that Ben has always experienced niceness as its own reward. *What can I do to help?* he asks. *Please, take mine,* he insists and smiles, and everyone says, "Oh, aren't you nice!" and "What a lovely young man!" (Or sometimes, "What a lovely young lady!") But I'm not all that worried about a boy being too nice. He still has the power and privilege of masculinity on his side so, as far as I'm concerned, the nicer the better.

Birdy, though. Birdy is polite in a *Can you please help me find my rain boots?* and *Thank you, I'd love another deviled egg* kind of way. She's fun in a scatological Mad Libs kind of way, laughing hysterically over "Goldilocks and the Three Turds." But when strangers talk to her she's like, *Whatever,* and looks away, scowling. She does not smile or encourage, and I bite my tongue so that I won't hiss at her to be nice to the creepy guy in the hardware store who is telling her how pretty she is. Do I really think it's a good idea for girls to engage with zealously leering men? I do not, so I swallow my own impulse to be liked. I try not to nudge. "Say *thank you* to the nice gentleman who wolf-whistled!" "Smile at the frat boy who's date-raping you!" I want my daughter to be tough, to say no, to waste exactly zero of her god-given energy on the sexual, emotional, and psychological demands of lame men—of lame anybodies. I don't want her to accommodate and please. I don't want her to wear her good nature like a gemstone, her body like an ornament.

And she's not really in danger of doing that. Even though her peers describe her as the nicest kid in class. Even though I catch myself thinking she should be nicer. Is that because her glower casts its gruff little shadow over my own good nature? Maybe. Or perhaps because the dignified solemnity of a girl makes people nervous—even me. At her age, I cartwheeled through my grandparents' living room, giggling. At her age I smiled and hugged all the people who spread their arms toward me, even if they were bona fide creeps. It's not what I want for Birdy, of course, but the impulse to please can be strangely hard to shake off. "Geez," I teased her last weekend when her expression was especially solemn. "It's like we're eating pizza in the morgue." She looked at me over her pesto slice, inched up a smile, abashedly, and I filled with regret. Why would I cajole her out of seriousness?

I love that she's so decisive and no-nonsense, with her short hair and soft pants with their elastic waistbands. Dresses get in her way, and don't even get her started on jeans, the snugly revealing allure of which completely mystifies her. ("What's so great about your crack sticking out all over the place?") She's the kind of person who donates money to the Animal Welfare Institute and attends assiduously to all the materials they send her, including their dully depressing annual reports, which she keeps in a special folder. "I'm done with down," she says, about her winter coat—which she will shortly replace with a synthetic one. "Here. Read this, about the ducks." ("Do I have to?" I stop myself from asking.) Gender stereotypes, among other injustices, infuriate her. "This is so stupid!" she sighs at Target, about the pink rows of dolls and the blue rows of LEGOs. "Why don't they just put a penis or a vagina on every toy so you can be completely sure you're getting the right one? A butt icon could mean it's a toy for everybody."

She is tender, fierce, and passionate. She can stroke our pussycat with gentle fingers while she growls at you, her eyebrows a menacing shelf, about bedtime and her plans to avoid it. Even as a two-year-old, she had the determined wrath and gait of a murderous zombie gnome, and we grimaced at each other, afraid, over her small and darkly glowering head. She will lift knife and fork, sighing, only if I scold her about eating with all ten fingers like a caveman, and I have mixed feelings about that. She cups ants in her palms and transports them gently from the kitchen to the garden so they won't be massacred with poison. She worries about the pantry moths. "Aren't they going to get sick from chewing through all that plastic?" she frets, while I check the flour for worms, toss the cocoa, clean up piles of shavings and husks. "Honey," I say, tired. "I'm more worried about our food than the moths." And she shakes her head judgmentally over my illogical heartlessness.

"She's very *moral*," a friend said recently, and it wasn't a compliment. She's the kid who can be a pain in the neck on a playdate, insisting on the rigors of turn-taking, of fair-sharing, of tidying up before the guests vamoose and leave her with an afternoon of mess to deal with. That said, she's got your back. She is a patron saint of babies and animals, of the excluded or teased. "That's not right," she's not afraid to say. "Stop it."

Which is what she does with "The Ali Mountain Song." "Do you know what Birdy wants to talk to me about?" the music teacher asks me. "She made an appointment to meet with me." "I'll let her tell you herself," I say, and smile. And she smiles back. Later, at the performance, the teacher introduces the song by explaining that two of the students have expressed a problem with the lyrics, and they're going to sing a revised version. Birdy and Keating beam through the altered chorus: "Ali Mountain boys are so very lovely, Ali Mountain girls are very, very strong," and then—you can't make this stuff up—they fist-bump.

I say a silent amen. Because god help me if that girl ends up moving through her entire life like she's smiling for tips. Or pole-dancing. Or apologizing for some vague but enormous infraction, such as the very fact of her own existence. I picture her at the prom in stripy cotton pajamas, eating potato chips with both hands. I picture her slapping a patriarchy-damning sticker on her jacket. I picture her running the country, saving the world, being exactly the kind of good bad girl that she knows herself to be. And I think: *You go.* I think: *Fly!* I think: *Take me with you.*

EPILOGUE

AND BETTER STILL

One day your baby will be turning twelve. Twelve! You will gather her up like a colt, trying to figure out how to contain all of her colt legs in your middle-aged lap. She will laugh and laugh, her face aglow like a lantern, like it's lit from within, even as your own face will be turning gray and sagging off onto the floor.

This daughter's hair, which has been defiantly boy-short for years, will grow into her eyes, down to her shoulders, and you will wonder about this. "Are you growing your hair?" you will ask her, and she'll shrug vaguely, say, "Maybe." You'll think about peer pressure. You will picture the tween girls in her class with their lace camis and black bras, with their hoochie-mama dresses, and you'll seethe. Your daughter is being coerced, forced to conform! Your heart will break a little. "It's for kind of a dumb reason," she will confess to you now. Then she will get out the Archie McPhee catalog of pranks and gag gifts and shyly show you the hairdo selector, with a spinner that determines your daily style: braid, ponytail, updo. "You need long hair for it," she says shyly, and you will realize for the millionth time that you really don't know anything.

At the kids' school, you will watch a father kneel down to comfort his preschooler, who is crying about stalagmites and stalactites. You will hear him say, seriously, "The different words about cave growths can be very upsetting," and you will turn away to laugh. As you sneak off, still laughing, you will hear the toddler add, cryingly, "Also *spelunking.*" You will realize that you have extricated yourself from the minutiae of your children's daily thoughts and feelings. Their psyches are where they live largely alone now, without you prowling around all hours of the day and night.

You will also realize, putting together a collection of essays about them, that the kids are no longer sick so inordinately often. Nor do you fear for their lives on an hourly basis. Thinking this, you will knock wood, in case fearing for their lives on an hourly basis is what's been keeping them safe all these years.

"We know, we know," the children will say, in unison, when you remind them about your drug policy. "We won't try meth or heroin or crack cocaine even one time." "Right," you will say, "because—" "Because it trashes your dopamine receptors. We know, we know."

Your first baby will be fifteen and his voice will drop five octaves over the course of the two months that he simultaneously grows three inches. Everyone will do a double take when he is suddenly looming in their doorways, sounding like James Earl Jones.

"Do you want to play Settlers of Catan?" he will ask, and you will say yes. Do you want to play cards or watch *The Office* or get takeout from the good Chinese place? Yes, yes, yes, you do. In three years he will be gone. Your daughter will still climb into your bed, sheepish, with a stack of picture books, and you will be glad. You don't believe me, because you are still reading the awful ones, like *Pooh Gets Stuck,* but you will be.

Your son will stand in the bathroom doorway with a smear of foam above his lip and a razor in his hand, chatting into your bedroom. You will put a finger in your book to keep your spot while your man-child fills the doorway with his tall, talking self. You will remind yourself to listen to the actual content, not just to the fact of his little lemon-drop voice getting buried alive in gravel. He will be confessing how he kind of still wants to have a job like in Richard Scarry's *Busy, Busy Town,* in a paper factory or a fabric mill or inside the enormous cross-sectioned engine room of a ship. "I mean," he will say, "believe me. I know those are all totally crushing jobs in real life. But still."

He will watch *The Possession, The Shining, The Birds,* with buoyant delight but looks on with frank, exaggerated horror when you pluck your chin hairs in the bathroom mirror. You can tell from his expression that every revolting thing in the world has been concentrated in the lower part of your face. When you catch his disgusted eye in the mirror, he reshapes his mouth into an apologetic smile. You stick up your middle finger and he laughs, leaves the room noisily beatboxing.

He will be full of sudden domestic judgments. "Does the kitchen sponge have to be so gross?" (Yes.) "The recycling smells." (Indeed.) "Didn't our floors use to be nice and shiny?" (They did!) Coming in from his monthly lawn mowing, he will manage to communicate more overheatedness than a supernova. He will flop on the couch, conspicuously fanning himself, and he will ask, breathless and, it would appear, having a small stroke, if you wouldn't mind getting him a glass of ice water. You will bring him the water, but you will say, "It's, like, ten square feet of mowing. I think you'll be okay." "You're welcome," he will say. You'll want to stay and argue, but you'll have to rush out instead to buy him pants, pants, and more pants. The getting of pants will be your new full-time job. If you listen hard in the night, you can hear the children's legs growing.

Speaking of the night: your son will no longer look like a baby while he sleeps. For years, even as his limbs stretched and dangled, his dreaming face regressed to the contours of infancy—downy cheeks; pearl of nose; the pink, pouched lips of a nursling. But now the face will chisel out its jutting new edges: brow and jaw, nose and chin. Like a Neanderthal crossed with a peach. His hair will reach past the middle of his back, but he will no longer be mistaken for a girl.

Talking to your angry daughter about her math homework, you will be distracted by cheekbones and beauty. Also by the pimple on her nose, flashing like a beacon. The message it will send you is *Hormones*. It will say *This too shall pass* or maybe *This is not a giant and preternaturally bewildering toddler, it's a person undergoing a neurochemical situation.* You will wonder suddenly if acne is adaptive. Maybe parents of clear-skinned cave children had no visual reminder of the fleetingness of adolescence, and so killed those children off. Maybe pimpled children survived to reproduce because the parents could see that they were temporarily possessed by glands and sebum. The parents understood that all they could do for this spotted person was leave out a tube of Oxy 10 and drive her to the good fro-yo place even though, yes, it was theoretically bikeable. You will wonder about this.

Meanwhile, the most important things the children have to say will have to be said with their lips clamped slurpingly around a Tootsie Pop. They will still laugh a lot over poop jokes. They will pass car trips in a complicated game of their own invention that will involve a ukulele and mandatory song-writing prompts. "World's Worst Penis Injuries, Volume Two," you will hear your son instruct, and you will hear your daughter strum a ballad that starts "You thought you'd cut your bagel..."

You will fold the children's clean clothes, and even though it won't be all the baby socks and miniature lamb-printed onesies, it will still make you feel like you're in love. The piles of worn T-shirts and long-legged jeans and striped pajamas. You will hold them to your chest and sigh. You love them so much! But also, there is so much laundry. You will wonder why the kids aren't washing their own clothes, and you will vow to get on that.

You'll get an e-mail from an old friend who's expecting a baby. "We just hope that everything is fine," he'll write, and this will make you shake your head, laugh a little cynically: it is a much less modest wish than your friend will think it is. Every day you will be thankful for ordinary days.

You will hold other people's babies with the buoyant confidence of an old grandma. "This is just a phase," you will say, patting the babies in your robust grandma way, while the new parents cry about teething or tantrums, while the new parents fall asleep on your couch. "It gets so much better than this," you will say to your exhausted dentist when he talks to you, defeated, about his toddlers. "It does, right?" he will say, gesturing to your sturdy, capable kids, and you will promise through a mouthful of gauze.

Your teenager will scramble into his enormous boots to take a walk when you invite him. The oak leaves on the ground are thick as leather, and they fill you with joy and sadness. These are the same oak leaves that the kids crunched through when they were chubby, staggering toddlers, proud in their brown lace-up shoes and knee deep in autumn. "I feel like we're just walking through the leaves, and the calendar pages are flying off, and we're already walking through the leaves again," you will say, and the teenager will say, "I know, right? Even *I'm* starting to feel like that." He will bolt away to look at something, then he will smile at you from a patch of sunlight. And it won't be so different from when the kids were two: all you can do is be there, open-armed and always, in case they turn. In case they run back.

Acknowledgments

O Dear, Dedicated Readers! Who have followed a column that morphed and migrated from "Bringing Up Ben" to "Bringing Up Ben and Birdy" to "Dalai Mama" and, finally, to "Ben and Birdy." You have kept me company, testified, and circled the wagons for more than a decade. Thank you.

My stunning agent, Jennifer Gates, combines devilish cheer-leading with angelic patience, and I'm so thankful to be in her care.

Laura Tisdel is the best editor, champion, and correspondent a person could be lucky enough to have; this is really her book. The whole team at Little, Brown has been pure sparkle and wit: Sabrina Callahan, Nicole Dewey, Carina Guiterman, Daniel Jackson, Deborah Jacobs, Jayne Yaffe Kemp, and the game, generous Vanessa Mobley.

In ways both direct and meandering, the pieces assigned to me by these writers and editors launched this book, and I'm so grateful for their wisdom and good faith: KJ Dell'Antonia, Andrea Buchanan, Judy Goldberg, Lygeia Grace, Caroline Grant, Lisa Harper, Julie Hogenboom, Noelle Howey, Catherine Kelley, Amy Maclin, Lindsey Mead, Cathleen

Medwick, Katie Motta, Jennifer Niesslein, Nicki Richesin, Linda Rogers, Louise Sloan, Marcelle Soviero, Allison Slater Tate, Jihan Thompson, and Stephanie Wilkinson. Also, everyone at *Wondertime,* especially Lisa Stiepock, Jeff Wagenheim, and Kathy Whittemore.

I would be nowhere without the steady work that I love. Thank you for keeping me shod and sheltered: Cheryl Brown, Daniel Hall, Ann Hallock (and the rest of the *FamilyFun* family), Elizabeth Passarella, Sally Sampson, and Kristin van Ogtrop.

Caroline and Tony Grant are models of creative generosity, and their Sustainable Arts Foundation grant made my life easier and better (sustainableartsfoundation.org).

And the people. The People! Who sustain me in both daily material ways and abstract emotional ways. All you Blum-Carrs, Corwin-Rosners, Elisons, Greenbachers, Michaelses, Perry-Greenes, Shahmehri-Costellos, Traphagen-Elkalais, and Walker-DelVicarios. Also my dear old friends Ann Hallock and Emily Todd. The "weirdies," Emily Bloch, Sarah Dolven, and Lydia Peterson. Lee Bowie and Meredith Michaels, Andrew Coburn, Judy Frank, Amity Gaige, Judy Haas and Gordon Bigelow, Daniel Hall and Pengyew Chin, Jill Kaufman, Sam Marion, Rebecca Morgan, Margaret Muirhead, Emily Neuberger, the Shannon-Dabeks, and the Todds. Plus the VanTaylors and Pomeroys, most of all Ali: late, great, and so badly missed.

I am grateful to Rob, Lori, Sam, and Lucas Newman, and to the extended Millner and Hunter clan for being such a fantastic family. Ted and Jennifer Newman are models of optimism and fretting, which makes me so glad they're my parents. Michael Millner does all the laundry—plus, he is the soul of patience, a barrel of monkeys, and the love of my life. Mwah! The fact that Ben and Birdy Newman are my constant companions might just make me the luckiest person in the world. They are brilliant, fierce, gentle, and funny, and I love living with them. This book is for you, my darlings, even though, yes, I technically dedicated it to your grandparents.

About the Author

Catherine Newman is the author of the memoir *Waiting for Birdy* and the blog *Ben and Birdy*. She is also the etiquette columnist for *Real Simple* magazine and a regular contributor to the *New York Times Motherlode* blog. Her first middle-grade novel will be published in 2017. She lives in Amherst, Massachusetts, with her family.